YORK NOTES

General Editors: Professor A. N. Jeffares (*University of Stirling*) & Professor Suheil Bushrui (*American University of Beirut*)

Arthur Miller

A VIEW FROM THE BRIDGE

Notes by Ian Milligan

MA, M ED (GLASGOW)
Lecturer in English, University of Stirling

**LONGMAN
YORK PRESS**

YORK PRESS
Immeuble Esseily, Place Riad Solh, Beirut.

LONGMAN GROUP LIMITED
Longman House, Burnt Mill, Harlow,
Essex CM20 2JE, England
Associated companies, branches and representatives throughout the
world

First published 1990
Sixth impression 1995

ISBN 0-582-02091-3

Typeset by Prima Graphics, Camberley
Produced by Longman Singapore Publishers Pte Ltd
Printed in Singapore

Contents

Part 1

Introduction

The life of Arthur Miller

Arthur Miller was born in New York in 1915 to Jewish parents whose fathers had both come to America from the same village in Poland. As a child, he lived in Harlem, which was then a fairly prosperous part of New York, where his father had built up a successful business in the garment trade. However, as he tells us in his autobiography, *Timebends* (1987), he felt he had absorbed 'two thousand years of European history, of which unbeknown to me, I had become a part', and that he had 'already been programmed to choose something other than pride in [his] origins' (*Timebends*, p.24). Applying for a library card at the age of six involved him in an interrogation about himself which made him conscious of belonging to a minority, whose institutions and customs seemed strange to him. Although it is written with hindsight and with the developed skills of a master dramatist, *Timebends* suggests that, even as a young boy, Miller was intensely aware of the differences between individual members of his family, and that he saw these differences as indications of types which were repeated generation after generation in the history of human relationships within the family. His childhood was full of stories in which the parts were played by his family and friends: these stories, as he tells them, had form; they expressed the character of those who took part in them, and it was their character which determined their fate. It may be that here we see the hand of the dramatist reworking his memories according to the habits of his later stage practice. On the other hand, we may observe in these childhood perceptions unconscious ways of seeing the world which were later to shape the fictional worlds of his plays.

When Arthur Miller was in his early teens, the New York stock market crashed and there followed the years of the Depression which affected many businessmen, including his father. The family had to move to Brooklyn, where Miller attended the local high school. The difficulties which they faced not only brought financial hardship but also damaged his father's reputation within the family; the impatience which Miller's mother felt for her husband's inability to surmount his financial problems shaded into 'a certain sneering contempt for him that filtered through her voice' (*Timebends*, p.112). Arthur Miller's mother's marriage had been arranged for her by her father; she had been a distinguished student at school and was an avid reader. His father was formally less well educated, but he had a keen interest in the theatre, and Miller came to respect his judgment about what he had seen. In *Timebends*, Miller describes the ambivalence of the family's feelings about his father: on the one hand, he was respected for his gentleness; on the other, he was almost despised for his lack of education and for his failure as a provider.

On leaving school, Miller felt under pressure to make money. He worked for a time in a warehouse which stored parts for cars, where he learned much about the hardship of the lives of working people, and where he had his first experience of institutionalised anti-semitism. He also made an attempt to become a singer. By this time he had heard of Marxism and had been introduced to the concept of world revolution. Drawn to the idea of comradeship rather than competition, Miller embraced a form of rational humanism, a viewpoint based on the belief that human destiny is determined by men and women themselves, rather than by any form of deity, and that conflicts can be resolved by intelligent argument and compassion. This outlook was opposed to the traditions of his family, and looked forward to building a new society out of the ruins of capitalism that Miller felt had failed his generation. To be interested in Communism in the 1930s, and to look optimistically to the Soviet Union as a model, seemed to Miller later to have been a rational response to his family's experience of sudden financial failure, even if events would show that he had been misled by his naivety.

In 1934 he enrolled as a student at the University of Michigan, which at the time had a reputation for liberal attitudes. There he intended to study journalism, though he later switched to English. While he was a student some of his plays won awards, including a prize given by the Theatre Guild in New York for student writers. In 1938 he graduated from university and spent a brief period working for the Federal Theatre Project, a Welfare Department organisation established to encourage playwrights, which he preferred to the bondage of writing scripts for Hollywood. In 1940 he married Mary Slattery, a Catholic girl whom he had known at university. They lived in Brooklyn, a borough of New York on the south-west end of Long Island. Little more than a week after their marriage, Miller went to work on a freighter because he wanted to get experience of life at sea, and also because he wanted to affirm that, although he was now married, he had not lost his freedom to explore the world. He talks of deep doubts within himself at this time and of his 'divided desire for settled order and a lust for experience that sent [him] off' (*Timebends*, p.70). He and his wife felt that they were consciously discarding the bonds of their respective religions and placing their faith in the humanist views Miller had earlier championed, whose best social exemplification, so they believed, was the Soviet Union. For a time he wrote radio plays, but he gave them up to work for nearly two years in the Brooklyn navy yard. In 1943 he left to make a screenplay based on a collection of newspaper columns by a popular war reporter. His first Broadway play, *The Man Who Had All the Luck*, which he began writing in 1941, was a failure when it was performed in 1944. Afterwards, Miller wrote that he thought the play contained the seeds of much of his later work; he had simply failed to develop adequately the relationship between father and sons and the conflicts between them. This theme was much more successfully explored in *All My Sons*, which was produced in 1947. In this play the conflict between son and father serves to demonstrate their duty to care for one another. The father commits suicide when he finally acknowledges his responsibility for the death of one of his sons. He also implicitly acknowledges a responsibility which transcends the family circle. The dead son stands for all the young men who have died because of the willingness of the older generation to profit from war. It is characteristic that Miller's response to the success of his play was to 'apply to the New York State Employment Service for any job available' (*Timebends*, p.138), so intense was his fear of losing contact with the people about whom he was writing and his sense of guilt at his success. It is also characteristic of him to confess that in the few days he then spent working in a box factory he found loneliness rather than comradeship.

Miller tells us in *Timebends* that in the years that followed *All My Sons* he began to explore the life of the waterfront in Red Hook, Brooklyn. He became interested in the lives of the longshoremen—the men who loaded and unloaded the ships—who led a precarious existence, knowing their jobs from day to day relied on the whims of unions and employers. In particular, he studied the disappearance of a longshoreman who had tried to challenge what he perceived as the corrupt leadership of the International Longshoremen's Association. Miller became involved in the political ambitions of one of the opponents of the union bosses, who hoped to increase his popularity among the Italian immigrant workers of Brooklyn by visiting their families in Sicily. Consequently, Miller embarked on a journey to Europe in the aftermath of the Second World War, where he became aware of the complexities of America's involvement in the reconstruction of nations which had suffered devastation and defeat. His experience of crooked labour leaders, with their connections with the Mafia, went into a screenplay, called *The Hook*, which was written for Columbia Pictures in 1951; but Miller refused to make his villains Communists, and the film was never made. His experiences nevertheless were to prove valuable, as it was from his involvement with the problems of the longshoremen of Brooklyn that *A View from the Bridge* would spring. But before *A View from the Bridge* was written there intervened, first, Miller's major success, *Death of a Salesman* (1949), an adaptation of Ibsen's *An Enemy of the People* (1950) and *The Crucible* (1953).

The post-war years in America were a time both of increasing tension with the Soviet Union and of a growing fear that Communism had become a subversive force in American society, especially in intellectual and artistic circles. The House of Representatives' Un-American Activities Committee was set up to investigate the extent of alleged subversion in public life and soon became a powerful and influential voice. A conference for world peace in which Miller participated during the first production of *Death of a Salesman* in 1949, which was convened to oppose the growing rift between America and Russia, quickly fell foul of anti-Communist sentiment in the United States. Miller himself had, by this time, begun to question the value of Marxism as a political dogma and of Russian Communism as a model for civil society. He was, however, totally opposed to the growing demands for social conformity and the harassment of left-wing political sympathisers. The following year he wrote a version of Henrik Ibsen's *An Enemy of the People*, which was intended to uphold the right of the individual to resist the pressure to conform.

According to Miller, this period of his life was one of personal re-examination, a process which influenced his first sketches for what he called *An Italian Tragedy*. The play set out to explore 'the mysterious world of incestuous feelings and their denial, leading to a murder-suicide' (*Timebends*, p.325), but as the political situation in the United States became dominated by the hearings of the House Un-American Activities Committee into the past political affiliations of writers, artists, film stars and so on, Miller decided to put the play on one side and turn to consider more topical themes. Struck by the atmosphere of irrational fear and unsubstantiated accusations that prevailed in 1950s America and by the parallel between the proceedings of the Committee and accusations of witchcraft which had been levelled against some of the inhabitants of Salem, Massachusetts, in 1692, he set to work on a new play, *The Crucible*. At the time of its first production in 1953 it was a critical but not a commercial success; it was not until later that it was performed world-wide to popular acclaim. In *Timebends* Miller notes that its popularity often seems tied to the political situation prevailing in the particular country it is performed: 'it is either a warning of tyranny on the way or a reminder of tyranny just past' (p.348).

Miller's opposition to the drive for conformity in his own country earned him considerable official displeasure which included the withdrawal of his right to travel abroad. In 1956 he was himself summoned before the House Un-American Activities Committee, but he refused to name those with whom he had associated at left-wing meetings in the 1930s, believing that while his views at that time might have been misguided, they had not been treacherous. As a result of his refusal to co-operate, he was fined and given a suspended sentence for contempt of Congress, although the conviction was later quashed by the Supreme Court.

When Miller was in Hollywood in 1951, working on his screenplay about the Brooklyn waterfront, he met Marilyn Monroe, at the time a young actress at the start of her career. During the next five years, as his marriage disintegrated, they kept in touch, even though she married Joe DiMaggio, the baseball star, in 1954. In 1955 the one-act version of *A View from the Bridge* was produced in a double-bill with *A Memory of Two Mondays*. The following year Miller divorced his first wife in order to marry Marilyn Monroe, and in the same year Miller and his new wife went to England where he was to work on a two-act version of *A View from the Bridge*, while she worked with Laurence Olivier on a film called *The Prince and the Showgirl*. The new version of *A View from the Bridge*, under the direction of Peter Brook, was a success, although it ran into trouble with the theatre censor because of its allusions to homosexuality, which was then a criminal offence in Britain.

Despite the almost universal adulation which she was now given by the public, Marilyn Monroe suffered from deep psychological problems which resulted in drug addiction. In 1961 she and Miller were divorced, and in 1962 Miller married Inge Morath, a professional photographer. He drew on her experiences in Germany during the war in his next play, *After the Fall* (1964). Unfortunately the play was interpreted by many as a painful exposure of his life with Marilyn Monroe, who committed suicide not long before the play was produced, and the coincidence of these events led to a fall in Miller's popularity which was not easily overcome. In *The Price* (1968) Miller returned to the theme of the rivalry between brothers and the search for events in the past which have determined the present. In *The Creation of the World and Other Business* (1972) he used the Old Testament story of Cain and Abel to show that fratricide had been one of the earliest memories of the Jewish people. Arthur Miller has continued to write plays which have been well received, though none has achieved the success of his earlier work. His later plays include *The Archbishop's Ceiling* (1977) and *The American Clock* (1980). In 1965 he was elected president of International PEN, an association of writers which has done much to break down barriers between East and West and to highlight instances of the suppression of freedom of expression. In 1978 he visited China where he later directed *Death of a Salesman*;

in 1986 he went to Russia and met Mr Gorbachev, the new President. In 1987 he published his autobiography, *Timebends*, which is both an account of his life and a political apologia.

A note on the text

Arthur Miller wrote two versions of *A View from the Bridge*. The earlier, one-act version was first performed as part of a double-bill with *A Memory of Two Mondays* in New York in 1955, and these two plays were published the same year under the title *A View from the Bridge: Two One-Act Plays by Arthur Miller*, with a preface by the author. Miller then reworked the text as a two-act play, and this is the version that is performed and studied today. It was first produced at the Comedy Theatre Club, London, in 1956, and was published, again with a preface by the author, the following year in *Collected Plays: Volume I* (Viking, New York; reissued by Secker and Warburg, London, 1974). There are a number of editions of the play currently available; perhaps the most readily obtainable is that published by Penguin in their Modern Classics series.

Part 2

Summaries

A general summary

Act I

Eddie Carbone, a dock worker, lives in Brooklyn with his wife, Beatrice, and her niece, Catherine, whom they have brought up. Catherine is grown up now and is beginning to look forward to a life of her own, but Eddie is afraid of the dangers she might face. He brings news of the arrival of Beatrice's Italian cousins who are being introduced illegally into the United States. Beatrice is excited but anxious; she is grateful for Eddie's generosity to her relatives. When Beatrice tells him that Catherine has got a job, he is upset and worried. He does not want her to be associated with the wrong people; he is also afraid that she will leave them. Eddie's worry about Catherine is not shared by Beatrice, who encourages her to make her own life. When Catherine expresses her fears for the safety of the immigrants, Eddie impresses on her the need for secrecy and Beatrice recounts the fate of someone who informed on a relative who had entered the country illegally. When her cousins, Marco and Rodolpho, arrive, they are welcomed by the family. The brothers look forward to making money in America, and Marco hopes to use this money to support his family in Italy. Rodolpho, who is unmarried, soon makes friends with Catherine, arousing jealousy in Eddie, who is distressed by the attention which Rodolpho is showing his niece. Beatrice for her part is greatly concerned by Eddie's distress: all his thoughts and feelings seem to be preoccupied with Catherine. As the young people fall in love, Eddie tries to separate them by suggesting to Catherine that Rodolpho is only interested in becoming an American citizen, which legally he would become if he married her. Beatrice strongly supports Catherine, advising her to trust her feelings, and pointing out the dangers of dependence on Eddie. When Eddie consults Alfieri, the lawyer who acts as the narrator of the play, he is told that he cannot prevent Rodolpho marrying Catherine, even if he does not approve of him. Nor does it matter if Eddie thinks he is not manly enough for his niece. He points out, however, that Eddie can choose to turn the illegal immigrants over to the authorities. That evening, when the family is discussing the life the cousins have left behind in Italy, Eddie directly challenges Rodolpho about his behaviour with Catherine. He believes that he should concentrate on work; having a good time might draw attention to him, and to his illegal status. Catherine's response to Eddie's aggressive behaviour is to ask Rodolpho to dance to a record they have bought, which arouses Eddie's anger. He offers to teach Rodolpho to box and, in doing so, hits him hard, hurting him. Rodolpho then asks Catherine to dance, and Marco, noticing his brother threatened, challenges Eddie to a test of strength in lifting a kitchen chair with one hand. Eddie fails to lift it, while Marco easily lifts it above his head.

Act II

Alone in the house just before Christmas, Rodolpho and Catherine play out a love scene, at the end of which Rodolpho leads his sweetheart to the bedroom. Eddie, returning home unexpectedly, soon suspects that they have been making love. Instantly he tells Rodolpho to leave. When Catherine tries to say she is going with him, Eddie brutally kisses her, as a sign of his authority, and then kisses Rodolpho, displaying his contempt. After another talk with Alfieri, Eddie impulsively telephones the authorities to inform on the brothers. At home he tries to re-assert his authority over Beatrice, who in turn tries to persuade him to accept Catherine's decision to marry. He is making a last attempt to persuade Catherine to change her mind, when the immigration officers arrive to find not only Marco and Rodolpho but two other illegal immigrants who have been living in a neighbour's apartment. Beatrice and Catherine are quick to see that Eddie has betrayed them. As Marco spits in Eddie's face, Eddie tries to defend his reputation. But Marco accuses him of killing his children by preventing their father from working. As the brothers are led away, Eddie threatens to kill Marco. Alfieri, the lawyer, is able to arrange bail for them, but he makes a condition that Marco should not take the law into his own hands by taking revenge on Eddie. It is clear that Rodolpho's impending marriage to Catherine will save him from deportation, but Marco will have to return. Back in his apartment, Eddie is still attempting to assert himself. He demands an apology from Marco and requires Beatrice to choose between him and Catherine, whose wedding he forbids her to attend. Catherine denounces him for his treachery, but Rodolpho arrives to warn them that Marco is preparing to take his revenge (despite his apparent promise to Alfieri). Rodolpho tries to save the situation by apologising to Eddie himself. But Eddie refuses to be reconciled with a man whom he regards with contempt; he insists that Marco should take back the devastating accusations he has made against him. Beatrice tells him that what he really wants is Catherine, and implores him to acknowledge the reality of his hidden desires. Eddie, however, refuses to agree that he has such thoughts. When Marco arrives, calling his name, Eddie goes out to meet him, defiantly defending his reputation. When he calls Marco a liar, Marco strikes him. When Eddie produces a knife, Marco turns it against him, and Eddie dies in Beatrice's arms.

Detailed summaries

Note: In the published text of the play there are no scene divisions in the two acts. For the purpose of these summaries, each act has been divided into the 'scenes' into which it naturally falls. These are identified by the opening and closing words of each 'scene'. The 'scenes' are numbered in square brackets.

Act I [Scene 1] (*The street and house-front of a tenement* . . . ALFIERI *walks into darkness.*)

The action is set in the living-room of Eddie Carbone's apartment in Brooklyn, which contains a rocking-chair, a dining-table and chairs and a portable gramophone. The set is not intended to be realistic: it is meant to represent the densely packed community of which Eddie's family is one unit. Outside the flat the street runs to the right and left. At the right is a desk which represents the office of Mr Alfieri, the lawyer. Nearby is a telephone booth. These locations and the items of furniture mentioned within the flat have a significant role in the action of the play. When it begins, we see two longshoremen, Louis and Mike, pitching coins against the building on the left. They nod to Mr Alfieri as he arrives at his office and he in turn opens the main action of the play by speaking directly to the audience. He comments on the uneasiness of the longshoremen in his presence. Lawyers and priests signify death to ordinary people: in Sicily, from where most of the neighbourhood has emigrated, the rule of law has not been effective for many centuries. As an immigrant of Italian descent, Alfieri remembers the lawlessness of New York in the 1920s, although he recognises that the idea of justice influenced even those who were gangsters. Now, New York observes the rule of law. Manners are moderate; there is no need for self-defence. Alfieri has spent much of his life engaged in dealing with the unromantic problems of the dockers who make up the population of the neighbourhood. But sometimes he does find himself confronted with a case which reminds him of the fiercer customs of Sicily or of the irresistible tragedies of the ancient world. As he leaves the stage, he notes the entrance of Eddie Carbone, a longshoreman who is to be the central figure in the story which Alfieri will help to tell us.

NOTES AND GLOSSARY:

rocker: a rocking-chair

phonograph: a machine that reproduces sound from a disc, a record player

longshoreman: a dock worker who loads and unloads ships

since the Greeks were beaten: after a century of antagonism between Greeks and Carthaginians, Sicily fell under the control of Rome in the 3rd century BC

Al Capone: American gangster (1899–1947), born in Brooklyn, who achieved notoriety as a racketeer in Chicago during the time of Prohibition (1920–33), when the sale of alcohol was illegal in the US

Frankie Yale: another gangster of the period

the greatest Carthaginian of them all: Carthage, an ancient African city, waged war against its neighbours in the Western Mediterranean but failed to conquer Sicily. Miller identifies Sicily with the Greeks and with ideas of law. Al Capone, being against the law, is presumably then identified with Carthage

Brooklyn Bridge: suspension bridge in New York City, and southern-most of the bridges across the East River between lower Manhattan and Brooklyn, built 1869–93

Red Hook: a section of the Brooklyn borough of New York City along the shore of the Upper New York Bay. Its port area includes the Erie and Atlantic shipping basins

Calabria: the toe of the Italian 'boot', separated from Sicily by the narrow Strait of Messina

Syracuse: capital of Syracuse province, south-eastern Sicily, originally founded by Greek colonists from Corinth

---

Act I [Scene 2] (EDDIE [*moving up steps . . . stares at the smoke flowing out of his mouth.*])

After a brief word with the longshoremen, Eddie enters his house and begins to talk to Catherine, his niece. She is wearing a new skirt and has done her hair differently. She has something to tell Eddie but wants to wait until Beatrice, Eddie's wife, comes in from the kitchen. Eddie's pleasure in his niece's appearance turns to anxiety as he thinks of the way men have begun to look at her. Some of this may be Catherine's fault: she sways as she walks, and her high heels draw attention to her. Eddie promised her dying mother that he would look after her and he wants to warn her against men. Eddie has his own news: Beatrice's cousins have landed from Italy and are to arrive at about ten o'clock that night. They are to enter the United States in the guise of members of the crew of a ship they have travelled on. Their arrival was not expected until the following week and Beatrice's joy is mixed with anxiety as she thinks how unprepared she is. Some of her anxiety stems from her sense of the strain which these visitors will put on Eddie. He worries that her generosity to them will be excessive, as it has already been to other members of her family in trouble. Yet he thinks it ought to be an honour to give a home to people who have lived in poverty in Italy.

Now the two women begin to break the news to Eddie that Catherine has got a job. He is reluctant to give his approval: Catherine has not finished school and she has not asked Eddie's permission. Catherine explains that the principal of her college has told her of a job that is available. As she is the best student in her class, he is prepared to allow her to take her examination at the end of the year, even though she will have been working. As Eddie suspiciously asks where the job is, Beatrice tells him how much Catherine will be paid. The women stress the advantages of the experience the job will offer, but Eddie dislikes the neighbourhood in which it will be located: Catherine will be too near the waterfront. He wants his niece to work in a nice office in a good quarter. Beatrice makes light of Eddie's worries: Catherine is not a child; she should be encouraged to take the job. Eddie has insisted that Catherine should finish school and take a secretarial course; now she should be allowed some independence.

Looking at Catherine's new hair-style, which reminds him of the Madonna, Eddie remembers the years of her childhood. As he gives her permission to take the job, Catherine rushes to embrace him. They are both moved, but Eddie hides his feelings. Catherine begins to imagine how she can improve the house with her money, but Eddie fears she will start to lose contact with them. Beatrice has never worked, so she cannot advise Catherine, in Eddie's view. He warns Catherine against being too trusting. Beatrice diverts the conversation by talking of the coffee which Eddie has been unloading. For a moment he thinks of the pleasures and surprises of the docker's life. Soon the cousins will be coming, and Catherine asks what she will say if people begin to comment on their presence. Eddie impresses on them that they must say nothing about these newcomers; people should be left to draw their own conclusions. The family must not admit that they are sheltering strangers. Eddie reminds Beatrice of a neighbour's son who betrayed his uncle to the authorities and who had to bear the wrath of the neighbourhood. In reply to another question, Eddie briefly sketches the methods used to bring illegal immigrants into the country: bribes are distributed and work is found by those who organise the entry. When Eddie reverts to the question of Catherine's job, his emotion is more evident. He declares he never thought she would grow up. She goes to get him a cigar from the bedroom. As he turns to Beatrice, who has been avoiding his gaze, the atmosphere changes. He wonders why she has been 'mad' at him lately. She tells him he is the one who is 'mad', perhaps implying madness rather than anger, but at that moment Catherine returns with the cigar and lights it for Eddie.

NOTES AND GLOSSARY:

giving me the willies:	making me feel uneasy
walking wavy:	walking in a sinuous, undulating way
candy store:	sweet shop
sidewalk:	a pavement for pedestrians
'all the girls':	Catherine is not just like anyone else; she is 'special'
You'll be mad at me:	you will be angry, resentful
stenographer:	someone skilled in taking shorthand from dictation
Buick:	a type of motor car, one of the early leaders in the American market
stool pigeon:	an informer; a spy for the police
confirmation:	the rite of initiation to a religion, in this case the Catholic faith
snitched:	turned informer
pieced off:	bribed
the syndicate:	the group which organised the entry of illegal immigrants

---

Act I [Scene 3] (ALFIERI: He was as good a man . . . *and the room dies.*)

Stage lights go up on Alfieri who commends Eddie for the decent regularity of his life. It is now time for the cousins from Sicily, Marco and Rodolpho, to arrive. They come with Tony, their helper, but he leaves them to make their entrance from the street, as they wonder at the apparent wealth of their American cousins. There are then halting introductions in broken English, with Marco speaking for both brothers. Now he realises that Eddie's house is not large; he says they will go whenever Eddie wants them to leave; but soon, Marco hopes, they will have a house of their own. Catherine, going to make coffee, is struck by the physical difference between the two men—one is dark, the other extremely fair. To her annoyance, Eddie breaks in to ask the cousins about their journey. He tells them that they will be expected to work on the docks to repay the money which was lent to them to come to America, although they have no experience of such work. At home they turned their hands to any work they could find. Rodolpho laughs as he describes the hardships of Sicily; Marco is more serious. He has been forced to emigrate because he has a family to support. Beatrice expects that he will want to go back to them, but Marco thinks they will be in America for some time. They are aware of the difficulties of finding work in America but they are overjoyed at the estimate Eddie makes for their future earnings, and Marco is moved at the thought of the help he may be able to give his wife. Catherine asks Rodolpho if he is married, but he says he has no money to marry. He does not mean to return to Sicily until he is rich enough to buy a motorcycle. Rodolpho is also a singer, and he prides himself on his ability to sing many kinds of song. At Catherine's invitation, he breaks into a popular American song which he sings in a high tenor voice. Catherine is enthusiastic, but Eddie intervenes, to warn that Rodolpho will draw attention to himself. When the singing stops, Eddie turns to Catherine. He notices she is wearing high heels, and sends her to her room to take them off. When she returns, she offers Rodolpho sugar for his tea. He is obviously as impressed by her looks as she has been by his singing.

NOTES AND GLOSSARY:

the Danes invaded Sicily:	the Normans, descendants of Norse invaders who had settled in France, conquered Sicily (1060–91)
to scramble:	to struggle for a livelihood in competition with others
Napolidan:	popular song associated with Naples
***bel canto*:**	a style of operatic singing characterised by rich lyricism and brilliant vocal technique
Paper Doll:	popular song, with words by Johnny Black
Garbo:	Greta Garbo (1905–90), American film actress born in Stockholm, best known in early films for her portrayal of sexual passion; her beauty had a classic quality

---

Act I [Scene 4] (ALFIERI: Who can ever know . . . *a familiar world had shattered.*)

Alfieri introduces the next scene with a hint that the cousins' arrival has made a decisive change in Eddie's life, which will give it a new, and troubled, significance. Eddie is tense as he mentions the time to Beatrice. He is worried about Catherine and Rodolpho, who are out at the pictures. Rodolpho's presence has had a strong effect on Catherine, and Eddie wants to know if she has told Beatrice about her feelings for him. Beatrice thinks Rodolpho is 'a nice kid', but Eddie thinks he is 'a weird', strange and effeminate. His habit of singing at work is an embarrassment, and Eddie does not like the way his hair is styled.

For the first time there is a hint that Eddie feels that Rodolpho is not manly enough to marry his niece and that Eddie does not mean to encourage their association. Beatrice wants to talk about her own problems. Eddie has not made love to her for three months and she wants to know if she has done something wrong. Eddie, however, refuses to discuss the matter. He returns to his worries concerning Catherine, but Beatrice argues that he is being too protective. He leaves the house and chats to some work-mates, who praise Marco for his hard work and Rodolpho for being humorous, leaving Eddie unclear as to whether they mean that he is amusing or ridiculous. Catherine and Rodolpho enter. They have been to the local cinema, though Rodolpho says he would like to see the bright lights of Broadway. He has been telling Catherine about the pleasures of living in Italy, but Eddie remains aloof. As Rodolpho leaves them, Catherine probes Eddie's mistrust of him. Eddie tells her he misses her company, now that she is out so much with Rodolpho. She wants to know what Eddie has got against him. When she tells Eddie that Rodolpho respects her, he replies that he is only interested in marrying her because he will then become an American citizen. Despite Catherine's protestations, Eddie criticises Rodolpho, accusing him of selfishness. Catherine refuses to listen: she is sure Rodolpho loves her. She rushes into the house, where Eddie appeals to Beatrice to deal with the situation. Beatrice has become suspicious about Eddie's motives; now she tries to deal with Catherine as an adult. Gently but firmly she suggests that Catherine must break away from her dependence on Eddie, who has never encouraged her to grow up. She even hints that Catherine's impulsive affection for Eddie has led her into behaviour which is not appropriate. She also admits that her criticism of Eddie might be construed as jealousy of Catherine. These suggestions are new and surprising for Catherine, but she begins to see that it is now time for her to break away from Eddie.

NOTES AND GLOSSARY:

Paramount:	cinema named after one of the most influential film studios in Hollywood
heeby-jeebies:	feeling of uneasiness
his regular hair:	normal, not dyed (another hint that Rodolpho is 'not right')
submarine:	in this particular instance, a slang term for an illegal immigrant
The Matson line . . . The Moore-MacCormack line:	names of shipping companies operating on the waterfront
Flatbush Avenue:	Flatbush was one of the villages incorporated into Brooklyn

Broadway:	famous thoroughfare of New York City, chiefly commercial for most of its length but entering the theatre district at Times Square

---

Act I [Scene 5] (ALFIERI: It was at this time . . . And so I—waited here.)

Alfieri introduces the next scene, in which Eddie, looking strangely moved, comes to consult the lawyer about his suspicions of Rodolpho. When Alfieri says he has no proof that Rodolpho wants to marry Catherine so that he can become an American citizen, Eddie claims to know that Rodolpho intends to stay, because he is spending all of his money, rather than saving it to return to Sicily. Eddie's next move is to suggest that there is 'something wrong' with Rodolpho: he is not manly enough to marry his niece. Alfieri suggests that the only interest the law might have in Rodolpho is that he is an illegal immigrant, but Eddie refuses to listen to this suggestion. The lawyer then warns him against loving his niece too much; it is time to let her go. Eddie reflects on the sacrifices he has made for Catherine. Now it appears that Alfieri is advising him to give her up to 'a punk'. Eddie is furious when Alfieri hints that his interest in Catherine may have sexual implications. After Eddie leaves the office, Alfieri reflects on his sense of impending tragedy and on his powerlessness to prevent it.

NOTES AND GLOSSARY:
a patsy: someone who is cheated or made the victim of a joke
Hoboken, Staten Island, the West Side, Jersey: areas of New York across the Hudson River

---

Act I [Scene 6] (CATHERINE: You know where they went? . . . EDDIE'S *grin vanishes as he absorbs his look.*)

It is after dinner in Eddie's apartment. Catherine has been hearing more about the lives of Marco and Rodolpho. They had been fishermen, but they had not become rich, since they did not own their own boat. Eddie and Catherine make it obvious that they know little about the background from which the cousins come, while Beatrice turns the conversation to Marco's family, who are benefiting from the money he sends them. Beatrice asks if Marco will go back to his family, gently discovering the strong feelings of affection and trust he has for his wife. This enquiry is in stark contrast to Eddie's brutal suggestion that Marco's wife might be unfaithful in his absence. When Rodolpho claims that sexual constraints are stricter in Sicily than in America, Eddie implies that Rodolpho has been too free in taking Catherine out without asking permission.

Although Beatrice attempts to support Catherine, Marco warns Rodolpho not to stay out too late. In Eddie's eyes the cousins have come to work; there is no room for pleasure in their lives. At this point Catherine puts on a record of the song with which Rodolpho has been most closely identified, and she asks him to dance. As they dance, Beatrice reflects on what she has learnt of the cousins' lives in Sicily. From this it emerges that Rodolpho can cook. Adding this ability to the catalogue of Rodolpho's less than manly qualities (he can also make dresses), Eddie asserts that there is no place for Rodolpho in the dockyards. As his anger begins to show, he invites Rodolpho to go to a boxing match with him, and then begins to show him how to box. Rodolpho is surprised when Eddie lands a sharper blow than he expected, and Marco watches the encounter doubtfully. When Rodolpho asks Catherine to resume dancing, Marco challenges Eddie to lift a chair while kneeling with one hand behind his back. Eddie fails to raise it off the floor, while Marco raises it above his head in an ambiguous attitude of friendly triumph.

NOTES AND GLOSSARY:
Coney Island: beach resort and amusement centre of South Brooklyn
Greenhorn: an immature or gullible person
They got a beautiful quartet, these guys: 'Paper Doll' was recorded by a quartet called *The Ink Spots*
you gotta block me: to 'block' in boxing means to obstruct an opponent's blows

---

Act II [Scene 1] (ALFIERI: On the twenty-third of that December . . . unless you wanna go out feet first.)

Alfieri introduces the scene, making the point that for the first time Catherine and Rodolpho have found themselves on their own in Eddie's apartment. Catherine's first words are light, but Rodolpho wants to talk about deeper matters. She puts to him the question that Eddie suggested to her: would Rodolpho want to marry her if she preferred to go back with him to Italy? Rodolpho's answer is an emphatic 'no': for him Italy means poverty, while America offers work. It would be no mark of love for him to offer Catherine the tribulations of poverty. Citizenship is valuable to Rodolpho; in its security he could exercise his talents freely, but he declares he has no intention of marrying Catherine merely to be an American citizen. When Rodolpho asks her why she is afraid of Eddie, she begins to talk of her affection for him and of her wish that Eddie and Rodolpho should be friends. She loves Rodolpho, but she finds it hard to break her relationship with Eddie, sensing that she has more sympathetic knowledge of him than Beatrice does. Rodolpho insists that Catherine needs to make her own life. They embrace, and he leads her towards the bedroom. Shortly afterwards, Eddie enters, calling for Beatrice; he is slightly drunk. There is a pause as first Catherine, then Rodolpho, enter. Their attempt to appear unconcerned fails; but when Eddie orders Rodolpho out, Catherine prepares to leave also. When she struggles as Eddie tries to stop her, he suddenly kisses her. Rodolpho protests that Catherine is to be his wife, but Eddie sarcastically asks him what he, Rodolpho, is going to be, and, making his point more brutally, suddenly kisses him too. Despite Catherine's pleas, he orders Rodolpho to leave without her.

Act II [Scene 2] (ALFIERI: On December twenty-seventh . . . EDDIE: I'll see yiz.)

Once again, Alfieri introduces the scene, with a sense of foreboding. He is conscious of his own helplessness. Now he is discussing with Eddie the fact that Rodolpho refuses to leave. Beatrice has suggested that the cousins should move into the flat upstairs, although no one appears to have told Marco about Eddie's recent struggle with Rodolpho. Alfieri argues that this contest has revealed nothing about Rodolpho, but Eddie still believes he has shown up his lack of manliness. He had intended to prove to Catherine that Rodolpho was unworthy of her, but Catherine has persisted in her intention of marrying him. He asks Alfieri what he should do, but Alfieri tells him he can do nothing. Catherine is free to do as she pleases: Eddie ought to let her go with his blessing. He has no moral or legal grounds for opposing her wish to marry, and he would be despised if he attempted to get rid of Rodolpho in any other way. Eddie's next action is to telephone the immigration authorities.

Act II [Scene 3] (EDDIE: Where is everybody . . . I'll kill him!)

Eddie comes back to his own apartment to find that the cousins have moved into the flat upstairs. He blames Beatrice for the cousins' presence in the house, reminds her of his rights there and of his sense of responsibility for Catherine. Beatrice reproaches him for humiliating Rodolpho and for the effect this has had on Catherine. Eddie repeats his view that there is 'something wrong' with Rodolpho. But there is something still to be settled with Beatrice, who has accused Eddie of failing her as a husband. He wants to hear no more of such talk. He denies her right to question his judgment and his authority as her husband. He defends his opinion of Rodolpho and recites the history of the sacrifices he has made for Catherine, who, he claims, is too young to know her own mind. But when Eddie says he is now prepared to give Catherine more freedom, Beatrice tells him it is too late. Catherine intends to marry Rodolpho the following week, since she is afraid he may be arrested as an illegal immigrant. Beatrice tries to make things up between Eddie and Catherine, and would be pleased if he went to the wedding. Eddie is moved to tears, but he finds it impossible to talk to Catherine. She is determined to marry, but he responds to her invitation to the wedding by trying to persuade her to wait, in the hope that she might meet other young men. Eddie is alarmed to hear that two other recently arrived immigrants are lodging upstairs. He urgently warns her to get the cousins new lodgings, just in case the newcomers have been followed by the immigration authorities. As they argue, immigration officers arrive to search the house. It is clear from what they say that they have been tipped off; it is also clear from the attitude of Beatrice and Catherine that they have both decided Eddie is responsible. The officers take the cousins away, despite the pleas of the women, and Marco suddenly breaks away and spits in Eddie's face. As Eddie tries to defend himself, Marco breaks away again with further accusations which make the neighbours turn from Eddie in disgust, despite his efforts to justify himself. He threatens to kill Marco for insulting him.

Act II [Scene 4] (ALFIERI: I'm waiting Marco . . .ALFIERI: Only God, Marco.)

Alfieri is interviewing Marco in prison in the presence of Rodolpho and Catherine. He is prepared to have Marco released on bail if he promises not to hurt Eddie. Catherine pleads with Marco to ignore Eddie and to use the time left to him to work, since he is certain to be deported, while Rodolpho will be able to remain in America after he is married to Catherine. Marco is reluctant to make any promises: Eddie has insulted his brother and denied him the chance to earn money to feed his family. He asks Alfieri what remedy the law provides him with for the damage Eddie has done to him, but there is none. Reluctantly, he assents to Alfieri's demands, as Alfieri reminds him that God, not man, is the ultimate source of justice. As Catherine departs to collect Beatrice for the wedding, Rodolpho embraces his brother.

Act II [Scene 5] (*The lights rise in the apartment* . . . CURTAIN)

Back in Eddie's apartment, Beatrice is preparing to go to the wedding. Eddie tells her that he will only approve of her going if Marco apologises. Catherine tells him he has forfeited the right to be listened to.

Beatrice decides to stay with Eddie, suggesting that they all share the blame for what has happened. Rodolpho enters to warn Eddie that Marco is praying in a church—a clear sign that he is asking forgiveness for what he is about to do. It would be best for Eddie to leave. When Eddie refuses, Beatrice pleads with him, reminding him that Marco is now behaving in the vengeful way one would expect from a Sicilian in these circumstances. Eddie still believes Marco has insulted him; he has no interest in an apology from Rodolpho. It is Marco who has damaged his reputation in the neighbourhood. As he rises to seek Marco, Beatrice tries to bar his way, telling him that what he wants is not an apology from Marco, but a relationship with Catherine which he can never have. As Catherine and Eddie react with horror to this suggestion, Marco can be heard from outside calling Eddie's name. Oblivious to the pleas of the others, Eddie takes up the challenge, accusing Marco of ingratitude and treachery. He wants a public apology from Marco and an admission that he has lied about him. As they grapple, Eddie produces a knife which Marco turns against him, killing him. He dies in Beatrice's arms.

Part 3

Commentary

The genesis of the play

Red Hook and the Sicilian connection

Arthur Miller has written a good deal about the way in which *A View from the Bridge* germinated in his mind. First of all, there were his associations with Italians in Brooklyn and in Sicily: in *Timebends* (p.199) he reminds us that during the war he had spent almost two years working in the Brooklyn navy yards, where he had had close contacts with the Italian workers and had come to know their families. He even records a discussion he had with one of his mates about a troubling, mildly incestuous dream the man had about his cousin (*Timebends*, p.201). To Miller's suggestion that the dream might indicate the man's strong feelings for his cousin, and that he might want to make love to her, the man replied, 'To her? Chrissake, I told you she's my *cousin*.' Perhaps we get a hint here of the utter lack of self-knowledge shown by the character of Eddie Carbone.

In addition to such involvement at a personal level, Miller later became caught up in the politics of the waterfront. He began to be aware of the extent to which the attitudes of the workers in Red Hook, Brooklyn, derived from practices in Italy. The dockers competed every day for jobs which were in the gift of the hiring boss. Such a system seemed to Miller to be both humiliating and open to corruption: it was as if the normal rules of American society no longer applied. As Miller implies, from the viewpoint of comfortable, middle-class America, watching the action, as the title suggests, from a remote and perhaps superior position, the practices of the waterfront must have appeared both alien and unreal.

Miller came to know some of the men who were trying to organise the dockers so that they could protect themselves from exploitation by the union which was supposed to represent their interests. He learned about the protection-rackets, the bribes and inducements that men were forced to engage in to obtain work. He was attracted by the possibility of being able to write about an enclosed world which had never before been taken as a subject for literature or drama. It was at this time that he first heard of the story of the longshoreman who had turned in two of his own relatives to the Immigration authority because one of them had become engaged to his niece.

Miller's first visit to Sicily came about because one of the union politicians whom he had befriended conceived the idea of increasing his popularity by visiting the families of men who now worked in Red Hook, Brooklyn. Even where these men had made new homes and families in America, their links with those they had left behind in Italy remained strong. Notwithstanding its defeat in the Second World War, Miller found Italy an energetic and demonstrative society, steeped in what he regarded as superstition. In a telling phrase, Miller describes his sense of the difference between Europe and America: 'Europe was full of relatives and in America the pull of the blood connection was gone' (*Timebends*, p.164). Also in Italy, Miller encountered Jewish refugees from concentration camps who were clandestinely waiting for a passage to Israel, and this encounter deepened his experience of man's inhumanity to man. In Sicily he found American gangsters who had been exiled by the American courts, and who undertook to help him and his companion with their search for the families of Brooklyn men. There, too, he tells us, he found the site of an ancient Greek theatre which inspired him with a feeling that social order and coherence might be possible even if every actual circumstance pointed to instability and decay. Some of these experiences must have influenced the writing of *A View from the Bridge*, especially the striking visual evocations of the physical presence of Sicily, the sense of the value of loyalty to the clan, the sense of its strangeness, its primitiveness and yet, perhaps paradoxically, its sense of order and law. And, of course, Miller was also strongly aware of its connection with the roots of drama in the ancient tragedies of Greece. In Sicily, too, he saw for himself the conditions of worklessness which, as he puts it, 'made monstrous the idea of their betrayal after they had succeeded in escaping this slow dying in the sun' (*Timebends*, p.177).

The incest theme

Miller's experience of Sicily was not the only autobiographical circumstance which went into shaping his play. In the aftermath of the success of *All My Sons* in 1947, he tells us that he became dissatisfied with the contradictions of his own life, especially with his sexual life. He brooded over the family as a source of emotional complexity. He had already isolated tension and rivalry between the male members of a family as a theme in his work; now he became aware of sexual rivalry within the family itself.

In *Timebends* (p.145) he tells us:

> With no more Freud than rumour brought me, I could afford to admit into consciousness what a bit more sophistication might have

caused me to suppress: I knew that somewhere behind my sexual anxieties lay incestuous stains that spread toward sister and mother. Playfully my mind would set up chessboard arrangements, the pieces being father, mother, brother, sister, each with different powers and rights-of-way, imperious in one direction while vulnerable and paralyzed in another. Regardless of how the game played out, it had to end the same way, in a confrontation with the father after I had picked off sister and mother and pushed brother beyond the reach of effective action. The father could move in all directions, and his decree of punishment, of course, was always death.

Although it begins with the idea of incest, this account of Miller's fantasies develops into a reflection on power. It bears a certain resemblance to the plot of *A View from the Bridge*, if we think of the play as a struggle between the strong young man (Marco) and the punitive father-figure (Eddie), after the weaker characters have been pushed to one side. The difference is that in the play there is no victor: suffering and death are the outcome for Marco and Eddie respectively. This notion of incest as an element, in some sense at least, of his own experience, continued to nag at Miller. When he saw an off-Broadway revival of the play in the 1960s, he tells us, 'I suddenly saw my father's adoration of my sister, and through his emotion, my own' (*Timebends*, p.325). Some of these perceptions may appear simply to be the result of seeing every family situation in terms of a Freudian analysis of family relationships, but in the passage quoted above from *Timebends*, Miller is anxious to assure his readers that his observations pre-dated his knowledge of Freud and that even as a child he was able to see his family in both real and metaphoric terms, as ordinary people and also as seducers or rivals or destroyers, the surface reality concealing a powerful and frightening myth. In a striking formulation he expresses some dissatisfaction with *All My Sons*, not because he feels that it is too realistic, but because he feels that it leaves 'too little space and time for the wordless darkness that underlies all verbal truth' (*Timebends*, p.144). Incest, then, may be more than simply a psychological aberration or defect. It may be part of the moulding forces behind the genesis of this play: it carries us into that darker realm of unconscious interaction between the characters which determines their surface behaviour and which both author and audience may be aware of, even if they do not fully understand it at the time. *A View from the Bridge* is in touch with these sources of 'wordless darkness', and that fact may account both for its power and for its long gestation in Miller's mind.

The politics of betrayal

Although they may appear to belong to the surface rather than the depths of the play, a few words must be said about the political circumstances that prevailed when the play was produced. As has been mentioned earlier, in the 1940s, and 1950s the House Un-American Activities Committee had vigorously prosecuted its investigation into alleged Communism in America. In his autobiography, *A Life* (1988), Elia Kazan, who directed *All My Sons* and *Death of a Salesman*, records how in 1952 the Committee demanded that espionage against the United States should be punished by death and criticised the film industry for failing to weed out Communists and for giving money to people in show-business who supported professional groups which were sympathetic to Communism. Kazan details his own involvement with the Communist Party in the 1930s and explains how he co-operated with the Committee to name those whom he believed to have been members of the Party. He also tells us how his decision to do this was regarded as an act of betrayal, and records the rumour put about by a journalist that Miller had sent him *A View from the Bridge* to show what he thought of those who informed on former Communists. He denies that there was any truth in the rumour: by this time Arthur Miller had already written his play, *The Crucible* (1953), as a comment on the political climate of the time and the atmosphere of irrational suspicion which had been produced by the Committee's activities. Obviously, *A View from the Bridge* deals with the theme of betrayal, but this does not mean that it is best regarded as a parable about the political events of its time.

The play in performance

Students of literature must always remember that reading a play is a quite different experience from reading a poem or a novel or a piece of prose. Plays are written to be performed before an audience which is alert to more than the words on a page of text. The spectator in the theatre is part of an exciting social event. His or her personal response is magnified by the communal reactions of the entire audience, whose attention is modified and concentrated by the darkness of the theatre, by the saturation of light on the acting space in front of them. Even the familiar lines of a well-known play will be transformed by being spoken by a particular group of actors who make the play their own by the actions and control and physical grace or power of their bodies, by the beauty and force of their voices and the intelligence of their delivery. Instead of a script which the reader painfully deciphers, moving clumsily from speech to speech, separating the spoken words from the stage directions of the playwright, the spectator hears and sees an uninterrupted sequence of words, actions and expressions, taking place in a setting which supports them, focused and heightened by the reinforcement of the lighting of the stage.

There is no substitute for such an experience in the theatre: students of plays must always remember that the printed page is only the basis of the play; it is from this set of printed symbols that the play will emerge, but it needs an act of concentrated imagination to bring it to life. How can the reader make this effort alone? One answer is that there is a theatre in the mind, and that the mind has ears as well as eyes. The solitary student is in the same position as the individual who undertakes to direct the play or to play one of its roles. The director has to be aware of the play in its totality, as a coherent sequence of visual and verbal meaning. Stopped at any moment, the play offers a group dynamic, a set of people caught in a complex relationship, which is a product of their history as individuals and as a group. In *A View from the Bridge* the established relationships of Eddie, Beatrice and Catherine, which are at a point of change at the beginning of the play, are subject to the impact of new habits of mind and expectations when Rodolpho and Marco arrive. One can see the relationships almost in terms of a chemical change: the bonded family trio is about to lose one of its elements; it is the new bonding between Catherine and Rodolpho which causes the first reaction on stage, followed by an even more explosive one, when Marco and Eddie collide according to the laws of a more primitive associative process—the vendetta—which unexpectedly erupts within a working-class family in twentieth-century New York. Audiences will, of course, be made aware of the steps which lead up to each of these climaxes, and of the psychological tension which precedes them, as well as the physical and verbal force with which they erupt. Directors and actors must, however, first be aware of the mechanisms of language and action, of attitude and gesture which cumulatively trigger these moments of intensity on stage and which may be all that their audiences will remember. To get anything like the effect of the play on stage, and to have any genuine understanding of its movements and rhythms, of just why it has been organised in this particular way, the reader, too, must make an analysis comparable to that of the director.

The reader/director, then, can stand, as it were, outside the play, searching its text for the logic of its action—for the sequence of events which lead to a final outcome. (It is not, of course, suggested that there is only one logical path to be found for the action of a play; in such open-ended structures there may be many). Miller quotes Peter Brook, the first English director of *A View from the Bridge*, as saying that 'the English tend to flee from Ibsen and the Greeks and anything else that shows some underlying logic to life, so that if one thing happens it is almost certain to cause something else' (*Timebends*, p.355). Presumably thinking of the British tendency to 'muddle through', he suggested that British people looked in life for 'a happy accident' to save them from their difficulties—and so, presumably, looked for it in drama too. Whatever may be thought about Brook's opinion, what he says reinforces the need to read the action of the play in a sequential way, to see it as a dynamic structure in which each phase of the mechanism produces a movement in the action. In practice, this means looking at the dialogue as a sequence of units, each of which has its own meaning and force. Such units may be marked by pauses or changes of tone or subject-matter, as the control of the conversations moves from character to character. At first, such shifts may seem to have negligible force: conversation may appear to veer aimlessly, moving from topic to topic; but suddenly we notice there is a direction. The pressure from each unit of the interaction between the characters pushes the play towards an outcome which begins to take a shape which seems inevitable. It is the special skill of the reader/director to notice currents of meaning within the play and to give them just enough emphasis to reveal the underlying sense of the action.

There is, of course, another way in which the play can be read which brings the reader into the heart of the action. He or she may read the play, not as a director, but as an actor. An actor, preparing to play one of the parts, will be most anxious to see how the continuity of his or her interpretation of the character can be realised. How can his or her appearance in one part of the play be linked to later appearances? It is not always easy to answer this question, if one is playing a minor character, whose scenes may be important, even if they are few and widely spread. (Think of Alfieri, for example, who has to be commentator and participant in this play.) What changes are forced upon the character by interaction with other characters in the play? Once again what the reader/actor is looking for is a logical development which will carry the character from the relatively open beginning of the part to its closed and seemingly inevitable outcome. Miller has laid considerable stress upon causation and motive in the action of his plays. In the preface he wrote to his collected plays, he says, 'I take it that if one could know enough about a human being one could discover some conflict, some value, some challenge, however minor or major, which he cannot find it in himself to walk away from or turn his back on. The structure of these plays, in this respect, is to the end that such a conflict be discovered and clarified.' Miller does not believe that there are no mysteries in life, but he says that the dramatist's problem 'is not to make complex what is essentially explainable; it is to make understandable what is complex without distorting and oversimplifying what cannot be explained'.

In describing the characters of the one-act version of *A View from the Bridge* in the preface he wrote for its publication in 1955, Miller wrote, 'There was such an iron-bound purity in the autonomic egocentricity of the aims of each of the persons involved that the weaving together of their lives seemed almost the work of a fate.' This quotation begs two questions: first, can the actor find such continuity in the way that Miller has written the lines for his characters that what they say and do seems to have a logical connection throughout the course of the play? The second question is more complex. The quotation suggests that each of the characters is so intent on his or her own purposes that he or she has no real knowledge of the others. Does that mean that to understand the play from the point of view of its characters will not be sufficient? The role of the reader/actor is incomplete. The play is not just the aggregate of its characters: it is the complex product of the unintended consequences of the words and actions of each character. For a complete view we are forced back into the stalls as director/interpreter of the text of the play.

Another point of view which should be borne in mind when we think of the play in performance is that of the designer who must provide its setting. Miller's brief stage directions at the opening of the play provide the essential details of the stage set, but choices must be made about how elaborate it should be. A painted backcloth of the Brooklyn Bridge might echo the title of the play and help to locate the setting of Eddie's house. More elaborately built sets might suggest that Eddie's apartment is only one of a warren of such apartments in the tenement block. If the set is constructed with a balcony which overlooks the central acting area where Eddie's apartment is built in outline only, we can be more aware that this block is populated. Figures may be seen looking over or going about their business until in the second act they are drawn into the action of the play as it moves beyond Eddie's family and affects his neighbours, bringing on him the condemnation of his society. The audience can look through the walls and windows of the front of the house, because the wall is built up to waist height only; they can see the entrances to the kitchen and the bedroom which at certain moments in the play are loaded with values associated with the two women and with Rodolpho. The side door to the left of the house is clearly outlined because it is a significant boundary between the private life of Eddie's family and the public life of which they are a part. Louis and Mike, who hang about the front of the stage which represents the public street, act as a kind of chorus, offering an informal view of how Eddie's peer group judges what is happening. Alfieri, whose place is to the right of the stage, has two roles: he is the voice of a social group which is superior to that of the other characters in the play, but which is nevertheless connected to them. His viewpoint is the view from the bridge which connects sophisticated and rootless New York to the Brooklyn which contains the uprooted underclass of Eddie and his neighbours. But Alfieri is also an Italian immigrant who can sympathise with his working-class clients, even if he is content to be distanced from them. In his discussion of *A View from the Bridge* in the introduction to the collected edition of his plays, Miller attributes the success of the two-act version of the play in part to the greater realism of its setting, so that Eddie is seen no longer as 'a kind of biological sport' but as part of an intelligible social situation.

The question of form

Miller has often spoken of the importance in this play of a controlled and structured form. He first saw the play as 'a one-act with a single rising line of intensity leading inevitably to an explosive climax' (*Timebends*, p.353). But although the play was first conceived in one act, the two-act version has an elegant shape. In the detailed summaries in Part 2, these two acts have been further sub-divided into scenes. Most of the transitions from scene to scene are managed by, or concern, Alfieri, who has a central role in controlling the action and in suggesting how the audience should appraise it. How far Alfieri's judgment is to be trusted will be a matter for further consideration, but it is probable that his view of the action is close to Miller's own. He opens and closes the play, overtly commenting upon the significance of the action. Each act of the play has, of course, its own structure. We have already noticed that there is a parallel between the acts in the number of their scenes. There are similar parallels in the plot of each act: in Act I the 'accidental' blow that Eddie lands on Rodolpho's chin and Marco's subsequent challenge to him over lifting the chair finds an echo in the violence later, in the second act. Eddie's kissing of Catherine and Rodolpho outdoes the boxing match in aggression, just as the final contest between Eddie and Marco unmasks the real feelings that may have been implied by the contest in the first act. It is worth noticing, too, how Miller almost immediately caps the act of violence towards Rodolpho in Act I by the double outrage at the beginning of Act II, which then becomes the first step in the train of events that leads to a fatal outcome at the end of the play. It is as if Miller has taken the ending of the first act and enlarged it; the shock of what happens at the beginning of Act II raises the temperature of the play and intensifies our expectations of what is ultimately possible. The violence which lurks under banter and joking has suddenly appeared in its native form, shorn of restraint and ready to kill.

We may readily grant that *A View from the Bridge* has a strong sense of line and climax, but nevertheless question the intrinsic value of its content. When Miller was in Sicily and saw the ancient Greek tragedies being performed, he admired 'the inexhaustible tension of their unadorned straight line to the exploding flare of consequences realized at last' (*Timebends*, p.175). In using similar phrases for the Greek tragedies and for his own play, does he imply that *A View from the Bridge* is a tragedy? In *Death of a Salesman* Miller had written one of the most successful tragedies of modern times. The principal character of that play represented the ordinary man whose aims in life reflected the false values of a commercial society. In his preface to the one-act version of *A View from the Bridge* (1955), Miller wrote about the problem of portraying a character in a society in which the organisation of modern industry has divorced the individual from the social group. He argued that in such a society people are seen only as functionaries. They have public lives as consumers or machine-tenders; it is only in their private lives that they have a fullness of being that can be treated dramatically. Miller believes that the question serious drama must answer is 'How are we to live?' To dwell only on the private, the personal, on the sexual pair or the family group will not answer this question in social terms. Optimistically, he concluded in 1955, 'It is now possible to talk of a search for values. . . with a warm embrace of mankind, with a sense that at bottom everyone of us is a victim of this misplacement of aims.'

To what extent does *A View from the Bridge* deal with such profound issues? For some, this play may seem to fall into the category of melodrama rather than that of tragedy. According to M.H. Abrams in *A Glossary of Literary Terms* (5th edn), the characters of melodrama are flat types: 'The plot revolves around malevolent intrigue and violent action, while credibility both of character and plot is sacrificed for violent effect and emotional opportunism.' If this characterisation seems too lurid to apply to *A View from the Bridge*, despite the violence of its climax, the play may nevertheless seem to have something in common with the *verismo* of some late nineteenth-century operas, which drew their themes from real life and emphasised naturalistic elements of the action. It may even be remembered that the most famous of these operas, Mascagni's *Cavalleria Rusticana* (1890), which ends with a violent and bloody clash between its two main male characters, is itself set in Sicily and is based on the theme of revenge. Miller's idea of the play having 'a single line of intensity leading to an explosive climax' does not in itself guarantee that it contains the depth of social analysis which he claims for it in his preface. It certainly implies that it will have a powerful effect on stage, but the attention of the audience may be held, and the emotions aroused, without the intelligence being wholly satisfied. Is *A View from the Bridge* a series of cleverly linked events, which increase in violence until the final blow is struck, or is it in fact a tragedy whose protagonist has been defeated by the false values to which modern society has made him adhere? In judging these matters, much will depend on our view of the stature which Miller has given to Eddie Carbone as a representative of the barely articulate working man whose finer instincts have been corrupted by a commercial society. It is not enough, however, to consider *A View from the Bridge* in terms of its origins or in terms of Miller's aim. The key to its significance lies in a careful examination of the text.

The testimony of the text

Act I [Scene 1]

The first scene of the play is Alfieri's ruminative, quizzical introduction. It serves to connect Alfieri with the local Brooklyn community, but we are also reminded of his social and professional distance from the people he serves. This play is a view of Red Hook from Brooklyn Bridge, a survey from a superior and alien standpoint of the values of a close-knit community. Alfieri was born in Italy; he is of these people, but he is distanced from them: 'now we are quite civilized, quite American'. He insists that Red Hook is not Sicily, and yet not long ago violent deeds were committed on these streets, similar to those of the Sicilian gangs. A significant theme in the play is the importance of the rule of law and the contrasts in opinion between cultures as to the definition of a criminal act and the recognition of representatives of legal authority. Alfieri represents a conventional idea of law which is rational, codified and explicit. Rationality and objectivity were attributes of Greek thinking which were opposed by the Carthaginians, who are seen in the play as enemies of law and order. Al Capone (1899–1947), the gangster who flourished in the 1920s, is here taken to be a representative of that lawlessness. Yet there is a paradox: even among gangsters there remains a notion of justice, which appears ambiguously related to law. Alfieri is glad that gangsterism has been defeated, yet there is a hint of compromise in his admission that 'now we settle for half'. It is a phrase he repeats in his final speech. Does it mean that the humdrum processes of law cannot approach the ideal of absolute justice? Does it mean that absolute justice is accompanied by a manifestation of divine anger with human imperfection which human beings would rather not contemplate? In this apparent mismatch between 'law' and 'justice', in the suggestion that there could be those who were 'justly shot by unjust men', there lies a thought that the conventional idea of law may not be enough.

In addition to setting the audience an intellectual puzzle, Alfieri sets the scene and introduces the main character, openly suggesting that Eddie Carbone—'this one'—is a modern instance of a universal

type and that his story will end in bloodshed. The speech is cleverly
written. Some of its lines clearly belong to the elaborate cadenced
'verse' in which it was originally written for the one-act version. But
this elaborateness grows naturally from its colloquial opening. It
suggests the balance which Miller has tried to strike between the
naturalistic and the symbolic. In some sense, Miller tells us, what we
are about to see is a modern instance of a perennial tale which is not
about an individual but about permanent aspects of mankind.

Act I [Scene 2]

The second scene takes us into Eddie's apartment. Alfieri's language
has been wide-ranging, meditative, extended, complex in structure—
the speech of an educated man. He is, of course, consciously
addressing the audience, and, although his tone is initially colloquial,
his status as a lawyer and his role as a commentator compel him to be
formal. The language of Eddie, Catherine and Beatrice is quick,
spontaneous and conversational; it is the unpolished vernacular of the
working class, used in privacy. It implies more than it states;
unsophisticated on the surface, its currents run deep. Its abrupt
simplicity hides unuttered depths of feeling, which are more likely to
be revealed in the gestures and body-language of the characters than in
the obvious meaning of the words spoken. There is no direction in the
script about the amount of physical contact there might be between
Eddie and Catherine, for example, but there is no doubt about the
vibrancy of Catherine's greeting to Eddie, and none about the
eagerness with which she displays herself to him. The first part of the
scene is devoted to Eddie and Catherine, and immediately currents of
attraction and dissension are set up. There is no doubt how much
Catherine values Eddie's approval, but, reading the speech with
hindsight (as we must do, seeing the future presaged by the present),
we notice the anxiety behind her ecstatic welcome of him. Catherine is
changed in dress and appearance: he sees her as 'the college girl',
approaching the ideal he has had for her. His reference to her dead
mother gives his appraisal of her an almost paternal note. His pleasure
in her appearance, with an exact and detailed scrutiny of her dress,
goes along with a fear of its effect on other men. Compliments and
criticism are inextricably linked: his awareness of her sexuality leads to
his first extended speech. Suddenly, he sees her in her new dress and
shoes as an irresistible attraction, which he can graphically express in
the simplest of metaphors. The 'clack' of the shoes and the turning of
the heads seem part of one machine, as if Catherine were playing into
the hands of the men who will pursue her. (The suggestion is implicit
in Eddie's words, even if they do not express it.) When he again raises

questions about Catherine's appearance and behaviour, he once more alludes to her dead mother, emphasising his sense of responsibility for her and her own immaturity. 'One of them girls that went to college' is also 'a baby' who does not understand 'these things' and yet is 'getting to be a big girl now'. Eddie sends contradictory messages to Catherine, warning her about other men, but excluding himself from the warning.

Catherine's careful preparations for telling Eddie her news are swamped in the news that he brings himself. Beatrice's entrance was to have been the signal for Catherine to speak; now she listens to Eddie. Miller has cleverly shown us Catherine's uncertainty about what Eddie wants from her; he has shown her dependence on him, and also the frustration this causes her. But Miller postpones any further development of this theme. Now Beatrice and Eddie are the focus of attention; perhaps it is a mark of Catherine's generosity of spirit that she completely forgets herself in her sympathy with Beatrice. Now Eddie is the confident master of the situation; he has no doubt about the security of the arrangements which have been made for the new arrivals; he is expansive, brushing aside difficulties. Beatrice is flustered and anxious, guiltily conscious of her shortcomings as a provider, forgetting how little these shortcomings will matter to the new arrivals. She is deeply thankful for their safe arrival—her strong sense of family is evident—but her generosity may be Eddie's loss. He jokes about the sacrifices he has previously made for her family, but there is a tension in their conversation which points to a hidden uneasiness. We scarcely expect Beatrice to say that it is Eddie she is worried about, unless she is unsure about his feelings. His jokes about her generosity unsettle her: can he really imagine himself in the immigrants' shoes? There is something abstract about the honour he feels in helping them. He can sympathise with their plight, but the unthinking generosity of Beatrice's response may come from 'too big a heart'. What are the limits of this man's kindness to strangers?

There is further evidence of Eddie's prickliness when Catherine's news is finally broken—by Beatrice, not by Catherine herself. The suddenness of it takes him by surprise: Catherine has failed to get his permission first. His reluctance to get excited survives her recital of the wholly favourable sequence of events which have led to the offer. Only the mention of her salary injects a note of excitement, as if he were seeing her in a new light as an adult wage-earner. But she is being drawn into a neighbourhood and into a social position which Eddie does not think is good enough for her. His intention is that she should 'get on': what he has groomed her for is success in the wealthy competitive world, not in the lower echelons of which he is a part.

In the sequence that follows Beatrice and Eddie are alone for the first time. Beatrice's surprising analysis is that the effect of Eddie's ambition for his niece is to keep her at home. If nothing is good enough for her, she stays as she is. But the job is an honour; it is already a measure of Catherine's success. Unpretentious as she is, Beatrice has put her finger on Eddie's perverse reluctance to be satisfied: he reacts angrily when she asks him if he means to keep Catherine in the house all her life, but it is a first glancing thrust at his possessiveness. Persuaded, Eddie softens into the maudlin: now Catherine is 'the madonna type'—too pure to be tainted by the company she might keep. In giving her his permission, his tone and gestures suggest new levels of shared intimacy. Now the actors must reveal the unselfconscious trust and affection they have felt for one another in the past, even if Eddie protects himself with smiles and unconvincing attempts at rough masculine incomprehension. For Catherine, a future is opening up which will free her generous spirit, but for himself Eddie foresees only loss.

Now his paradoxes appear awkward contradictions: Catherine has 'learned bad' from her 'good aunt'; and 'most people ain't people'. The relaxed warmth of love within the family is at risk if it is exposed to the world, which is eager to dishonour and destroy it. Once again, it is contradictory to see the world both as a source of honour and as the place where value is destroyed. For a moment Beatrice changes the mood by allowing Eddie to romanticise the world of work he has just presented in such harsh terms. The coffee that Eddie unloads can smell like flowers, even if there may be spiders amongst it. Now the atmosphere on stage is mellower as the pleasures and romance of work are acknowledged. Anxieties about Catherine shade off into less intense anxieties about the immigrant cousins, but there is a continuity of theme. The cousins will be safe, provided they remain within the protection of the family which will conceal their presence from the outside world by a wall of silence. Above all, they are not to be talked about: people who see them can draw what conclusions they please. At this point, the foundation parable, as it were, of the play is told—the story of the boy who 'snitched'—a word which evokes the horror children have of a broken rule or a secret betrayed. Beatrice tells the tale, conveying the horror of the breach of the unwritten code which the community has adopted for the preservation of its own: 'and they spit on him in the street, his own father and his brothers. The whole neighbourhood was cryin'.' Beatrice's words have an almost biblical simplicity as they suggest the absolute revulsion of the group for the individual who has betrayed it. But Eddie reveals another side to Beatrice's picture of pure group loyalty: these breaches of the immigration laws are in fact based on a sophisticated system of bribery. The syndicate which finds the immigrants work is concerned with them only while they pay off the debts they have incurred in being introduced to the country: group loyalty is adulterated by greed and racketeering.

In the episodes we have just considered, two of the major themes of the play have been initiated and cleverly alternated: first, Eddie's relationship with Catherine; second, the relationships between immigrants who have already settled in America and those who wish to enter the country illegally. The second is not unconnected with the first: the first is simply an instance of the primal group, the family; the second raises the question of how extended that group can become. For Beatrice, it seems, the claims of blood, however remote, are paramount; Eddie is more aware of the need to compete. He is more aware, perhaps too aware, of boundaries, beyond which other men are enemies.

The rest of the scene forms a tiny coda to what has gone before, reinforcing our perception of the poignant sense of attachment and loss Eddie feels for Catherine. Even as he gives her his blessing, they are still eagerly playing games of mutual dependence, as she runs to fetch him his cigar, a rather faint symbol of his masculine power. Left alone for a moment with Beatrice, we observe the tension between them and the anger that Beatrice has not yet been able to express or even to understand. Alfieri closes the scene with a comment which ignores these complexities: from the outside Eddie is an average citizen. And so he introduces the next scene, in which the immigrants arrive.

Act I [Scene 3]

Even as the cousins enter, we notice the differences between them. Marco is reserved; Rodolpho is exuberant and excitable, as well as egotistic. It is Marco who takes charge, establishing his relationship with Beatrice by recognising the tie of blood. It is she who makes the introductions, naming each time her relationship to the person she introduces. Marco is carefully profuse with his thanks, deferring to Eddie's right to determine how long they will stay. He instantly grasps the problems they might cause their hosts, looking forward to the time when they can have a place of their own. Catherine lingers to wonder at the physical differences between the cousins, but Eddie cuts her off sharply enough to hurt, and takes over the conversation from his rocking-chair, steering it away from Rodolpho's looks to the practicalities of their journey and the work they mean to do. Their cultural differences are immediately obvious; neither side understands the other's way of life. Rodolpho tries to convey what it is like to live in Italy, drawing the women back into the conversation. In contrast to Eddie's poverty of expression, which conceals feeling under everyday talk, Rodolpho's language is alive with detail; the simple metaphors he uses are vivid enough to make his talk seem different from the work-oriented world of the Carbones. When Beatrice appeals to Eddie to share in the world Rodolpho is evoking (with a 'how do you like that?', which is the best she can manage to express her pleased surprise), Eddie switches to Marco with a question about the length of their stay. While Rodolpho's sketch of Italy has been comic, Marco expresses the distress of bringing up a family in poverty and the pain of leaving them behind. Marco speaks simply, directly, warmly, the power of his feeling contained by the formality of his manners. His reticence is in marked contrast to Rodolpho's mercurial spontaneity. Both men are overjoyed when they realise how much money they will earn, and Marco's emotion at the possibility of helping his family is heartfelt. Already, Beatrice and he are on first-name terms; now, he wants to thank Eddie, and for the first time he addresses him with a formal Italian version of his name. But Eddie brushes his thanks aside with a question about the coffee, which is used throughout this episode as a way of diverting attention from any seriously threatening feeling. This scene emphasises the differences between Eddie and Beatrice; she is warm, sympathetic, imaginative; he is 'manly', objective, distanced, asking questions which are unsettling, if not threatening.

Now Catherine directs the conversation back to Rodolpho, giving him the chance to offer views of his naive dream-world. Asking him if he is married suggests her own unguarded impulsiveness; obviously, she thinks he is attractive. He is confused, imagining himself rich, but not able to see himself as more than a message-boy. Even Eddie is drawn into Rodolpho's imaginative world, though he is disconcerted to find that Rodolpho is also a singer. (Notice how tactfully Beatrice goes for the coffee, leaving Catherine to listen to Rodolpho's tale.)

Catherine is silent as Rodolpho imagines his triumphs as a messenger on a motorcycle and recalls his success as a singer. When he exaggerates, Marco is there to correct him, gently but firmly. When Catherine finds that Rodolpho likes jazz and popular American songs, her enthusiasm reaches a peak. But once more Eddie, ignoring her, brutally destroys the romantic mood Rodolpho has created. His song of romantic possessiveness is uncomfortably relevant to the relationship between Eddie and Catherine. We have been given enough insight into Eddie's reluctance to let her go to believe that she might well be seen as 'the paper doll' he does not intend to let other fellows steal. Brutally cutting through Catherine's excitement, Eddie tries to frighten Rodolpho with the possibility of exposure. It is Marco who rises to quieten Rodolpho. Eddie's 'they got guys all over the place' is the first vague threat that someone may report their presence in the house.

Eddie has regained the initiative. He has silenced Rodolpho; now he criticises Catherine's new shoes, suddenly making an issue of what she has been wearing since he arrived home. These are the shoes that he feared would make men's heads turn. That he criticises them now is a clear sign that he has seen the flash of sexual attraction between Catherine and Rodolpho, and it has made him angry. His attempt at humiliating her does not affect Rodolpho. His line, when Beatrice finally produces the coffee, is 'Sugar? Yes. I like sugar very much'—the words of an innocent sensualist to whom none of the pleasures of life is alien. As Catherine adds the sugar to his coffee, a bond is sealed between them, and the moment is not lost on Rodolpho.

By this point, Miller has begun to develop the two main strands of dramatic action in the play. The more difficult—the relationship between Eddie and Catherine—is the more carefully handled. The 'letting-go' of a child is not an unfamiliar situation, but Eddie's feelings seem stronger than is usual. Beatrice's comments on his attitude suggest a conflict within her which has yet to be developed. And there is a further conflict within Eddie himself: he wants Catherine to justify his life by realising his rather vague social aspirations, but he also wants her to remain where she is. The second strand of the action is what will happen to the immigrants. The possibility of their betrayal, however unthinkable it may be, is signalled in the second and third scenes of the play. Eddie's feelings about them are in conflict. He is himself the son of an immigrant, but he has been completely assimilated into his new milieu. He has no obvious interests outside work and family; he responds to none of the invitations to play baseball with his neighbours, and he has no contact with the musical culture of Italy. His duty to the cousins comes through Beatrice; he feels no sense of kinship with either of them. When Rodolpho admires Catherine, the two strands of the action dangerously touch.

Act I [Scene 4]

In his introduction to the fourth scene of the play, Alfieri's language bears further traces of the elevated language of the original one-act play. Here he is most obviously acting as the chorus of a tragedy, one of whose conventional themes was the undesirability of deviating from the common lot. The scene is broken into three or four episodes. The first is a dialogue between Eddie and Beatrice: she is relaxed, philosophical, even fatalistic when the possibility of the cousins' discovery is raised once more. Clearly, the relationship between Rodolpho and Catherine has moved on, and Eddie is troubled. He is fretting that the young people have not returned home, although we may think that eight o'clock is not late for an evening's outing to the cinema. Beatrice's attitude to the young people is very different from Eddie's: she sees only Rodolpho's positive qualities—his good looks, his capacity for hard work; she is sympathetic to the fact that Catherine is too excited about Rodolpho to put all her energy into her new job. Miller has written Beatrice's speeches here so that she can project relaxation and ease: it is as if she is trying to soothe Eddie into unconcern. Notice how much repetition there is in the speeches, and how Eddie repeats Beatrice's phrases with a different tone, matching her assurance with pessimism and concern.

What worries Eddie is Rodolpho's lack of conformity: there is something odd—almost unnatural—about his tendency to burst into song. Indeed, singing itself seems almost incomprehensible: 'a whole song comes out of his mouth—with motions.' There is something disgusting about Rodolpho's willingness to expose himself to the mockery of the men on the dockyards. Words such as 'weird', 'canary', 'Paper Doll' (applied to Rodolpho himself) suggest the doubt about Rodolpho's masculinity which is to become Eddie's main charge against him. (Rodolpho is 'like a chorus girl or sump'm' and his hair may be bleached or dyed.) As Eddie makes these suggestions, Beatrice's tone changes sharply, just at the point where she says, 'You crazy or sump'm?' At that point her voice has a new intensity, an edge of criticism we have not heard before, as she turns these charges against Eddie himself. She nips his aggressiveness in the bud, first by refusing to agree with him, then by turning the conversation to their own relationship. Once more, the depth of expression here depends on the tone which the actress uses: Miller's words are vague, even banal. The terrible phrase, 'When am I gonna be a wife again, Eddie?', characteristically emphasises Beatrice's relationship to Eddie and the rights that go with it. The question is direct and uncompromising, but it has no hint of hostility. Beatrice is wounded and reproachful, but she does not lose her dignity. Eddie's faint attempts to explain his loss of interest in sex lead back to the cousins and to Catherine. He 'don't feel good'. But to Beatrice's direct question ('You don't like me, heh?'), he responds with incomprehension. The poverty of the language used here does not conceal the seriousness of the breach in the relationship, but it fails to explain it. It clearly shows how ignorant Eddie is about himself and how stubborn he is in his refusal to admit that anything is wrong. It also shows what limits there are to Beatrice's power: however impressive she may be to the audience, she cannot break through Eddie's self-absorption. He keeps talking about the unsuitability of Rodolpho's interest in Catherine, whereas Beatrice wants to talk about the impropriety of his own. But her words are too imprecise to make the point and she has to be content with such phrases as 'I don't like it' and 'it ain't nice', without specifying what it is that she means.

The encounter that follows is an odd one: for the first time there is real contact between Eddie and his neighbours. As we have come to expect, the conversation is elliptical and allusive, pointing to possibilities which the speakers cannot put into words. Its teasing is open-ended, leaving the work of understanding to the audience. Miller divides the little scene between Louis and Mike, allowing Louis to initiate the conversation but leaving its disquieting development to Mike. The force of the scene arises from the unease it produces in Eddie. There is, first, the suggestion that the immigrants get work more easily than the residents. There is, of course, an allusion here to the manipulation of the allocation of jobs and the pay-off which the manipulators expect from it. The men's simple-minded comments about Marco and Rodolpho echo Eddie's earlier opinions, though they are milder in tone. Their inarticulate attempts to describe Rodolpho are ambivalent: the sense of humour they praise in him makes them behave oddly, as if his unconventionality rouses feelings they cannot handle. It is not clear whether he is being laughed with or laughed at. The intensity of their hysteria has a touch of malice which embarrasses Eddie, and may puzzle the audience. It is just enough to raise the temperature for Rodolpho's return.

In the third little section of the scene, Catherine and Rodolpho cap the laughter of the longshoremen with their own excited laughter. They have not so far broken bounds by going across the bridge to Manhattan, though this is what Rodolpho wants to do. The mood of pleasure which Catherine and Rodolpho share is vulnerable to the easily aroused hostility between Catherine and Eddie. Interested only in where she has been and in what she has been doing, Eddie is quick to be censorious. He is incapable of entering imaginatively into the naive picture that Rodolpho has of New York, as he projects the assumptions of Italy on to the landscape of New York, which is for him a bright world of theatre and opera, while for Eddie it is a world of danger. Rodolpho's fantasies and memories are meaningless to Eddie, who is interested only in Catherine and the unfulfilled claims he has on her. He is looking for the little girl he has lost; she is looking for his approval of the young woman she has become. These cross-purposes breed hostility. When Eddie accuses her of not listening to him any more, there is a wistful exchange between them, which consists of virtually the same repeated phrase:

CATHERINE: . . .What's the matter? You don't like him?
  [*Slight pause*]
EDDIE: [*turns to her*]: *You* like him, Katie?
CATHERINE: [*with a blush but holding her ground*]: Yeah. I like him.
EDDIE: [*—his smile goes*]: You like him.
CATHERINE: [*looking down*]: Yeah.

Moments like this are of great significance: as we have seen, these inarticulate characters do not communicate in explicit language. Yet this is an act of quiet self-assertion on Catherine's part: the effort which it costs her has to be expressed in her tone of voice and the 'body language' she uses, including her distance from Eddie and her eye contact with him, which Miller has suggested in the stage directions. Catherine's shy admission of an interest in Rodolpho, quite different, we may guess, from any she has previously felt for a man, signals a break with Eddie. When she follows up with 'You're like a father to him', it is a reminder of the gap between them, which he keeps trying to annul. What is now required of him is that he should give the girl he has brought up as his daughter to a younger man, but he refuses to see Rodolpho as a man of goodwill. Rodolpho's friendly overtures are ignored; Catherine's positive reports of his gratitude and of his respect for her are rebuffed with contempt. Glibly rationalising his possessive feelings, Eddie offers a sketch of a completely self-interested Rodolpho, oblivious of his relatives at home and prepared to deceive Catherine in order to become an American citizen. His picture is based on a highly selective number of facts and finds no echo in Catherine's experience. Any reply that Catherine offers is swiftly incorporated into Eddie's view of Rodolpho's intentions. Now, Rodolpho is a member of an 'out' group, an untrustworthy 'they', who ruthlessly exploit the opportunities available to them in a new country. The two themes of the play—incest and immigration—have become even more explosively embroiled.

This exchange between Catherine and Eddie has great force: it repeats the movement of the first episode in the scene between Eddie and Beatrice, beginning with relaxed banter which becomes more tense as the conflict between the characters is exposed. It divides into three 'movements': at first Catherine is dominant, quietly asserting her love for Rodolpho; but when she asks Eddie what he has against the young man, she allows him to build up a formidable, if purely hypothetical, case against him. Where Catherine sees love and affection, Eddie sees ruthless calculation. The irreconcilability of their respective positions becomes clear and brings the sharpest conflict yet between them—a rapid flurry of verbal blows, of assertions and denials. Catherine does her best to shut out Eddie's view of things; he is pierced by her desperate assertion of Rodolpho's love for her. At the end of the encounter, Catherine is in retreat, but Eddie is exhausted. When he turns to Beatrice for support, expecting her to 'straighten [Catherine] out', he meets another accusation, 'When are you going to leave her alone?'

On the face of it the words are unexceptionable; it is the vague, non-analytic language that we have come to expect from this household. When Beatrice follows up with 'or you gonna drive me crazy?', it is clear that her desperation springs from something more deeply personal than concern for her niece. For a moment, she is the wounded and neglected wife accusing her husband of unwelcome attentions to another woman. Once again, she and Eddie fail to communicate: she is registering anger and alarm at Eddie's behaviour, though she cannot find words to explain what she thinks is wrong. He can concentrate on judging Rodolpho, completely closed to the idea that it is his own behaviour which is in question. The stage direction tells us that Eddie walks out of the house 'in guilt', but are we to suppose he has a clear idea of the nature of his guilt?

In the episode that ends this scene, Beatrice and Catherine are left to confront one another. For the first time in the play, insight, self-knowledge and rationality replace blind instinct. There is a striking change in tone: Beatrice is searching but compassionate; Catherine becomes painfully aware of the strong sentiment which continues to bind her to Eddie. Perhaps for the first time, we learn that the attachment between them is not one-sided. When Catherine asks, 'What am I going to do, just kick him in the face with it?', the stage direction suggests she speak the line 'as one who herself is trying to rationalize a buried impulse'. We may infer that this means that Catherine wants to break free, and is secretly prepared to respond with violence to Eddie's assertion of parental rights over her. On the other hand, the buried impulse may be quite different: to imply that her love for Rodolpho will be like a kick in the face is perhaps to suggest that she does not want to hurt Eddie by admitting her love for Rodolpho. Perhaps her feelings for Eddie have deeper roots than she is aware of, or perhaps she is unwilling to relinquish the comfort that the relationship gives her.

Beatrice has no doubt about Eddie's inability to let Catherine go; she has already (in the first scene of the play) patiently catalogued the excuses Eddie has found for preventing Catherine's leaving home. Now she begins by gently encouraging Catherine to choose for herself and to be firmly self-assertive, but she grows less patient as she tries to expose the mutually satisfying, but wholly immature, bond that links uncle and niece. It is not surprising that her closely detailed list of occasions when Catherine has forgotten she is no longer a child begins to sound, even to herself, like jealousy. The audience must be acutely aware of the keenness with which Beatrice must have observed the sexual undertones of Catherine's intimacy with Eddie. Catherine's confused acceptance of the new knowledge Beatrice gives her is genuine enough, but her lack of insight into her own behaviour seems to mark a reluctance to begin a more adult phase of life: to cling to a substitute father may be safer than to throw in her lot with an attractive, but imperfectly known, lover. Beatrice's role in this scene is impressive: she is wiser, more experienced, yet gently sympathetic to the girl whom she recognises as a serious rival for her husband's affection. But behind the gentleness is a deep determination that Catherine should release them both from the stifling effects of Eddie's obsession. Perhaps for the first time in the action, language is used with a precise communicative force. Beatrice's 'Honey. . .you gotta' is lucid and determined: Catherine is not to be allowed to cling to Eddie. She must say farewell to her emotional dependency and embrace her new life with strength and dignity.

Act I [Scene 5]

In the next scene Alfieri adopts a new role by taking part in the action, but his introductory words help to reinforce the last impression we had of Eddie:

> . . .His eyes were like tunnels; my first thought was that he had committed a crime, but soon I saw it was only a passion that moved into his body, like a stranger.

The first phrase of these lines was in the one-act version of the play where it read:

> The eyes look like tunnels
> Leading back towards some ancestral beach
> Where all of us once lived.

In that context Eddie's eyes remind us of the long history of human tragedy and of the deep-rooted human emotions from which it springs. In the new context it can only suggest the narrowness of Eddie's obsessions. Perhaps we are meant to notice that an unimaginative lawyer may think it is less troubling that a man should be possessed by demons than that he should have committed a crime. That Eddie has long been 'taken over' by a passion suggests that his self-ignorance has moved into a deeper and more dangerous phase.

Now, Eddie's claim to know Rodolpho's intentions is insistent: his line, '*I know what's in his mind*', must surely be uttered with force enough to frighten. In this state of certainty he attempts to persuade the sceptical lawyer that his suppositions are facts. He argues that illegal immigrants save their money because they fear discovery, but Rodolpho spends freely. This suggests that he has no fear of deportation, because he knows he will marry. Alfieri is unimpressed: there is nothing illegal about an intention to marry an established citizen. There is, of course, a complete contrast between Eddie and Alfieri: one is insistent, emotional, anxious to persuade; the other is calm, rational, analytic. Even in this scene, we are presented with a contest. Eddie wants to use the lawyer as a substitute for the law itself; if he can convince Alfieri that he has a case, perhaps the law will be on his side. But Alfieri is not to be moved: Eddie cannot clothe his own prejudices in the objective force of law. Eddie's objections to Rodolpho are expressed in a torrent of emotion which finally suggests that it is Eddie, not Rodolpho, who is 'not right'. To Rodolpho's blondness— Eddie calls it 'platinum' to make us think of brassy, Hollywood cover-girls—and his physical frailty, his interest in music, his tenor voice (for Eddie a sign of effeminacy), has now been added an interest in dressmaking. Disturbingly for Alfieri, who is moved to protest, Eddie finds Rodolpho attractive, if disgusting:

> I mean he looked so sweet there, like an angel—you could kiss him he was so sweet.

The words are contemptuous, but the thought expresses a wish we should not expect Eddie to entertain. He describes the derision his neighbours feel but fear to express, reminding us of Mike and Louis's excessive and ambiguous laughter, but what maddens him most is the thought of 'that guy layin' his hands on her'. Lurking obscurely is the unexpressed thought that Catherine is deserting a real man (Eddie) for a fake (Rodolpho). The passion which inhabits Eddie's body is a smouldering sexual jealousy which no insight illuminates. We know that what Eddie has put into words—the wild suggestion of the kiss—will be bizarrely enacted in a later scene. In this way Miller both prepares us for the later event, and marks a stage in the progression of Eddie's disintegration: what is now a thought will later be acted out. As Alfieri insists, the only legal sanction that exists to stop Rodolpho becoming Catherine's husband is the possibility of his arrest as an illegal immigrant. Eddie recoils from the slightest hint that he might betray the cousins, but his initial appearance of incomprehension and the strength of his denial suggest that his mind is divided.

When Alfieri turns from questions of law, his advice echoes Beatrice's: more delicately than Beatrice he suggests that Eddie's feelings for Catherine are excessive. He is careful to speak generally and impersonally. He stresses, with genuine understanding, how excessive feelings towards a loved one unaware of their implications can create serious emotional problems. From his own experience, Alfieri knows the pain of parting from a loved female child—the sexual nature of the bond is tacitly accepted—but 'those things have to end'. A notable element of Alfieri's speeches is their sympathy and insight. He has abandoned the impersonal role of the lawyer. If anyone can come close to Eddie, perhaps, it is this man. Eddie responds, but it is with a bitter self-pity. There is nothing individual or unusual about Eddie's tale: he has sacrificed himself for his child and now he feels he is being robbed. Eddie's justification of his possessiveness is deeply unattractive; all the latent suspicion of the outsider boils over into hatred: Rodolpho has come 'out of nowhere', he has 'dirty filthy hands', he is a 'goddam thief'. Eddie has reached the point where his easy liberalism roughly collides with his self-interest. When Alfieri begins to lose patience, driving home the impossibility of Eddie's desire for Catherine, Eddie abruptly refuses to listen. Just as the law has been deaf to the turmoil of Eddie's feelings, so he is deaf to Alfieri's exposition of the rules that govern the intimacy of relations between male and female family members.

However banal Eddie's self-justifying outburst may appear in linguistic terms, it powerfully expresses the angry self-righteousness which marks his quasi-incestuous feelings. His emotions are rooted in a past for which he can never be compensated. The sacrifices he then made for Catherine have given him permanent right of possession over her. He has no idea that his cries of pain are unreasonable; all he knows is that his heart is broken. It is left to Alfieri, acting once again as a chorus, to confirm the spectators' view that such selfish ignorance must have evil consequences.

Act I [Scene 6]

The final scene in the first act takes place in the thoroughly domestic situation of Eddie's living-room. The extended family has just finished dinner: it is as if the action had regressed to the earlier harmony of the night of the cousins' arrival. Once again Miller builds the scene towards a climax by dividing it into smaller segments. This easy, drifting domestic scene is tightened and focused by the spurts of Eddie's anger, touched off in each instance by Rodolpho. The scene begins casually: as Beatrice and Catherine clear the table, Catherine happily imagines what life has been like for Rodolpho in Italy. But she is sensitive to the unspoken scepticism of Eddie, who characteristically takes over the conversation. Soon it is men's talk about boats and nets and money. Only those who own the boats in Italy make money: even in their own country Marco and Rodolpho have been excluded from work. For the Americans it is difficult to imagine such a different way of life. Beatrice grapples with the problem of imagining sardines as uncanned living fish; Catherine tries to think of the distant European countries the cousins have visited. The first note of anger is sounded when Eddie talks of the oranges he thinks may have been painted. In exposing his ignorance, Eddie reveals the depth of the cultural divide. Marco's reply is grave and formal; Rodolpho's has just enough edge to spark off Eddie's rage.

Successfully heading off dispute, Beatrice steers the conversation back to the satisfaction Marco takes in providing his family with money. But underneath there is the pain of separation, scarcely mitigated by letters from home. Beatrice's sympathetic enquiries about Marco's family are spoiled by Eddie's coarse jokes about infidelity. Once again he challenges Rodolpho, when he contrasts Italian strictness with American freedom in the relations between the sexes. As Beatrice is quick to notice, it is Rodolpho he means when he talks of 'greenhorns' who fail to understand the rules which govern the behaviour of young people in America. As usual, Eddie exaggerates: Rodolpho 'didn't exactly drag [Catherine] off', but the inexact phrase, implying a brutality unthinkable in relation to Rodolpho, is meant to suggest the degree of consideration Eddie expects for himself. He is also forced into contradiction when he says, 'I mean it might be a little more free here but it's just as strict.' What he is trying to express is the fact that the rules of American behaviour are signalled less obviously than those in Italy, but they operate with as much force.

Tortuously and indirectly, the question of Catherine and Rodolpho's relationship is now being faced. Marco thinks it can be settled by their coming home earlier; Beatrice wants Catherine to stand up for herself; Eddie tries to enlist Marco's support in heading off Rodolpho. Once more he raises the spectre of discovery and reminds them of the terms on which he accepted them. Both had come (in Eddie's view) to help Marco's family in Italy: he strongly implies that there is no place in America for an independent male who wants to make a life for himself.

In the awkward pause that follows, Catherine makes her own response by putting on the record that has become Rodolpho's theme tune and asking him to dance. If Eddie thinks he has made a new contract with Marco about Rodolpho's behaviour, he is mistaken. Supported by Beatrice, Catherine quietly asserts her own right to choose. The conversation uneasily reverts to the cousins' life in Italy, revealing Rodolpho's skill as a cook, another sign of what Eddie regards as his unmanliness, and leading rapidly to Eddie's counter-challenge. This time Eddie's words are more controlled; his ironic self-deprecation is in reality a mocking attack on Rodolpho, and his anger is expressed by the contemptuous ease with which he tears the rolled-up newspaper, as if it were a substitute for Rodolpho, the Paper Doll, himself. Now he tries to drive a wedge between the brothers. Rodolpho is unexpectedly addressed as 'Danish', as if he were not even a real Italian, and boxing is to be a final test of manliness, though it has not been a part of either brother's previous experience. The scene reaches a measured climax as Eddie lures Rodolpho into a trial of strength. Notice how Beatrice's initial suspicion of this aggression is converted to an enthusiastic admiration of the camaraderie which is supposed to exist within the sport. The scene is played almost in slow motion as

Eddie overcomes Rodolpho's reluctance even to feign aggression. Catherine picks up Beatrice's initial alarm, expressing it at a sharper level of anxiety. When Eddie's blow lands, only Rodolpho sees that it demands a response. Catherine rushes forward to defend her boy; Marco is not yet convinced that anything objectionable has happened; Beatrice is placatory. But Rodolpho has restarted the record and taken Catherine into his arms. Very slowly, Marco now responds to what he has decided has been an unfriendly act. In challenging Eddie to a trial of strength with the kitchen chair, he makes it clear that he is unshakeably loyal to his brother, and that in any real contest between him and Eddie he would win. Once more, Miller carries the play forward by offering a modified version of the action which will follow. Now also, for the first time, we see the male strength of the Italians, which emerges without emotion to convince us of its reality. As Marco holds the chair above Eddie's head there is no sense of threat, but merely a hint of the power which he could unleash if he chose to.

Act II [Scene 1]

After Alfieri's laconic introduction, which has a touch of sardonic humour, the second act continues with a lyrical love scene between Catherine and Rodolpho. It is the first time we have seen the sweetness and firmness of Rodolpho's character. Almost at once he expresses the warmth of his affection for Catherine, who is able to talk to him about her feelings of fear for Eddie and of her fear of love itself. The main purpose of the scene is to lay to rest any suspicion there may be in the audience's mind that Eddie's accusation, that Rodolpho merely wants to become an American citizen, may be true. Rodolpho wants to marry Catherine because he loves her, and he wants to become an American because he wants to work. Firmly, even passionately, he dispels Catherine's romantic ideas about Italy, pressing home the misery and evil of poverty. When he tells her he would not marry her if they had to live in Italy, he is able to say it without making his love for her appear shallow.

In addition to his evident impatience for marriage, Rodolpho persuades us of his honesty by the frankness with which he discusses his situation. He would indeed be a thief if he took Catherine to Italy, stealing from her both youth and beauty. He tells her frankly that he is not attracted by America, but simply by the possibility of obtaining work there. It is still an awkwardness in his position that it is only by becoming a citizen through marriage that he will obtain work, but he is clearly thinking of his future as one shared with Catherine. Why does she allow her fear of Eddie to postpone their wedding?

Now it is Catherine's turn to explain herself. There is a tender aspect to her relationship with Eddie. She has not meant to hurt him, and she cannot face the pain that she seems to be causing him. She is aware that some of Eddie's sadness comes from the failure of his marriage, and she is inclined to blame Beatrice for part of this failure. Reflecting on the sadness of growing up, Catherine evokes our sympathy. She shows an almost maternal tenderness for the misery of the man she knows so well and whom she will now be forced to leave. Rodolpho is equally tender: once again Miller has given him a simple but telling metaphor to express his thought. It is a repetition in gentler terms of Beatrice's 'You gotta' in the fourth scene of Act I. Rodolpho's gentleness and sense of responsibility are equally evident as he leads Catherine into the bedroom for her initiation into womanhood.

One of the most significant aspects of this part of the scene is that Rodolpho and Catherine have provided an ampler and more humane idea of what it is to be a man and a woman than anything Eddie or even Beatrice has been able to provide. The difference is underlined by the drunken brutality of Eddie which follows. His kissing of Catherine and Rodolpho demonstrates a new level of violence: his drunkenness allows him to release a verbal and physical rage which they respond to in the same spirit, although they cannot match the power of Eddie's contemptuous attempts to dominate them. When the rage has spent itself, there remains the threat to kill or to expose the illegality of the cousins' position. From now on they are dependent on Eddie's 'pity', and Catherine is out of bounds. The limits to Eddie's tolerance have been clearly set. In this final contest with Rodolpho he clearly thinks he has demonstrated what manliness is and has asserted his authority over Catherine.

Act II [Scene 2]

In his introduction to the next scene Alfieri reverts to the quasi-poetic language which he used after his first meeting with Eddie. Alfieri attempts to justify his status as an observer by maintaining that nothing had yet happened that would have forced him to act and that, in any case, he felt powerless to act. He appears to be a curious mixture of doctor and lawyer: he knew at the time that Eddie was struggling with serious problems, but until Eddie acted on his destructive impulses, he claims to have had no duty to fulfil. Miller uses Alfieri to increase the sense of the inevitability of tragedy, but he destroys his credibility as a participant in the drama. It is difficult to accept that he should have known so much about his client and yet have done nothing to prevent the adverse outcome which he feared.

Eddie's second interview with him does nothing to enhance Alfieri's moral standing. The point of the scene seems to be Eddie's rational justification of his bizarre action in the previous one. It is perhaps worth noticing that nothing is said about his kissing Catherine. His treatment of Rodolpho was a demonstration that he was 'no good': he did not fight back. Alfieri reiterates his view that Catherine must be allowed to make her own choice, but he also seems to foresee what Eddie's next move will be. As the phone booth begins to glow, signalling that Eddie is about to betray the cousins to the authorities, Alfieri warns him of the consequences of such an action. The scene, however, does not advance our knowledge of character or situation. It is mainly a narrative device, allowing Eddie to move from the threat of betrayal to the act of betrayal. Eddie's action has been well prepared for by the many hints that such an action was possible, but we are left without any insight into why Eddie decides to act now.

Act II [Scene 3]

Eddie's anonymous telephone call to the authorities brings him immediate feelings of guilt. His brief encounter with Louis and Mike illustrates the easy comradeship which he is about to forfeit. The scene that follows echoes this note of emptiness (Eddie's first words are 'Where is everybody?'), which is further emphasised by Beatrice taking down the Christmas decorations. It is the beginning of the final section of the play, in which the train of events Eddie has set in motion finds a final response from the cousins and from the community. At first, it looks as if Eddie has won: Beatrice has retreated into sullen acquiescence; she and Catherine have arranged for the cousins to go upstairs; Eddie has reasserted his right to rule over his own household. Once again, he sounds the note of blame which was first heard as a joke in the second scene of Act I: Beatrice's generosity has brought him trouble. But the removal of her cousins has not restored what he thinks is due to him. What he now demands from Beatrice is an unqualified acknowledgement of his rights as a man. She must accept his decision to eject Marco and Rodolpho; she must accept that he is right about Rodolpho's character; she must accept that he has the right to decide about their sexual relationships. Although she dutifully accepts his decision, she does not accept that he is right.

It is difficult for the audience to feel sympathy for Eddie. He is unconvincing when he asserts that Rodolpho is not 'right', while defending his own rather curious sexual abstinence. It is also difficult to believe that Eddie feels secure: his petulant self-assertion gives way to childish reproach as he accuses Beatrice of not agreeing with his judgment, as a wife should. He clearly believes in the infallibility of his intuition. He has brooded over what has been implied about his feelings for Catherine; now he wants it to be known that he has always acted for her own good. Pathetically, Eddie has regressed to a position which is no longer sustainable. He is still attempting to behave as if his word is law, offering concessions when his opinion no longer matters. Catherine's arrangements to marry Rodolpho are already in hand. As Beatrice gently leads Eddie to accept the situation, the theme of betrayal is sounded. The currents of the play are troubled and divergent at this point: the audience is suspended between the possibility of a resolution between Eddie and Catherine and the uneasy expectation that Eddie's telephone call will have terrible consequences. When Eddie begins to get alarmed that the cousins are going to share rooms with other illegal immigrants, we can see that he is afraid that what he has done will spread further than he intended. We may infer that the reason he gives for his alarm is precisely opposite to the truth. He is afraid that when the immigration authorities come to pick up Marco and Rodolpho, they will find neighbours' relatives as well. Soon he is in the grip of panic. The tempo of the play has moved from the gentle hopelessness of Eddie's attempt to persuade Catherine to behave as if Rodolpho had never existed, to an agitated and apparently irrational demand that the cousins should leave the apartment as quickly as possible. Only the audience can sense Eddie's fear of what is likely to happen next. As Catherine and Eddie swing back to a mood of direct opposition, the immigration officers burst in.

The spoken words of the next short section of the play have little significance: our attention is focused on the anger and disgust of Beatrice and Catherine, as their suspicion of Eddie's part in the cousins' discovery turns to certainty. His characteristic reaction is to deny knowledge and responsibility, but the fact that the officers know their address, coupled with Eddie's reasons for betrayal, points to Eddie's guilt, which finally shows in his face. It is at this point, perhaps, that a resourceful director would want to bring in the wider neighbourhood as Beatrice and Catherine ineffectually protest against the indiscriminate strength of the law, while the officers bring down Marco, Rodolpho and the two unnamed immigrants. Miller makes it clear that the officers themselves have Italian roots, though they are instruments of a law that operates without making allowances for the ties of blood. There follows a beautifully constructed chain of challenge and counter-challenge, as Marco, suddenly emerging as the representative of a different concept of justice, spits in Eddie's face. Eddie counters with his threat to kill, again behaving as if he does not know why Marco is blaming him, which Marco answers with the serious, public charge that Eddie has killed his children by denying him the possibility of work. The scene is constructed like an operatic quartet: Marco denounces; Eddie justifies himself; Catherine, having drawn Rodolpho out of the mêlée, continues her feeble attempts to foil the arrest.

Act II [Scene 4]

The scene that follows in Alfieri's office clarifies the action further: now we begin to see how the play might end. Marriage will provide a happy ending for Rodolpho and Catherine; but Marco will be sent home. The mood of this scene is highly charged, but it is in complete contrast to what has gone before. Public hubbub has been replaced by the sober calm of the lawyer's office. The business in hand is the matter of an application for bail for Rodolpho and Marco, but the underlying debate is whether Marco has the right to kill Eddie. Alfieri will not apply for bail unless he promises not to do so. Catherine pragmatically suggests that he can earn more money as long as he is free; Rodolpho wants him to be free for the wedding. Marco is not satisfied: Eddie has broken a primitive law which regulates the behaviour of kinsfolk, and therefore he ought to die. It is implied that Marco feels bound to execute this sentence, not only because Eddie has hurt him, but because all who recognise their absolute duty to help their kin have a duty to punish those who have failed to do so. But these concepts have no place in the criminal law of the United States. Marco denies that statutes enshrine the whole of the law, but Alfieri asserts that no individual can assume the role of God.

In this short but powerful scene, Miller has given an embodiment to two different ideas of law. A primitive notion of family ties which favours particular groupings is contrasted with an objective conception of justice which treats everyone alike, provided they belong to the same nation. What we see in *A View from the Bridge* is a clash between concepts of nationality and concepts of family, tribe or race which may transcend national boundaries. In this scene, which is an essential preparation for the final confrontation between Marco and Eddie, Miller allows Marco to speak of the principles which underlie his devotion to his family, which has been evident throughout the play. He does not do so in any connected or theoretical way. He simply expresses the profound conviction that a man's attempt to support his wife and family is a fundamental value and that these family ties have an almost religious significance. If these values are not embodied in the law, the law is defective. There ought to be sanctions against those who transgress them, or depreciate them, as Eddie has done. In some circumstances it would be dishonourable not to kill the man who has offended against the obligations families owe to one another.

Although Miller provides Alfieri with an equally powerful opportunity to contradict Marco's view of what is lawful, there is an ambiguity about Marco's promise not to touch Eddie which leaves the way clear for the final events of the play. Is his final 'All right' a promise not to kill, or is it an acceptance of the view that justice lies in the hands of God, not man? There is a solemnity about Alfieri's 'Only God, Marco', but it does not even raise the question of how God's justice is to be delivered.

Act II [Scene 5]

For the final scene of the action of the play Miller returns us to Eddie's apartment, where Eddie continues to nurse his grievances. Having failed to stop Catherine's wedding, he now tries to prevent Beatrice from attending it. Once more, the theme of family loyalty is sounded. Beatrice intends to go out of respect for her sister, Catherine's mother; Eddie's interest is completely self-centred. His wounded vanity demands assuagement: he wants 'his respect', apparently a last acknowledgement from his wife of his authority. There is no doubt that Catherine's breach with him is final: she speaks to him with a harsh bitterness of language which is new. She does not disguise her contempt for Eddie. Now that Eddie has shown what he is prepared to do, he has lost any right to respect: he is 'a rat', who belongs in the garbage. It is difficult, perhaps, to sympathise with Beatrice's view that they are all responsible in some sense for what has happened. No doubt she implies that Eddie's betrayal of Marco and Rodolpho is linked to the unhealthy relationship between Eddie and his niece, to which all the family have contributed, even if only by failing to recognise it for what it was. It is difficult, however, to believe that such considerations mitigate Eddie's personal responsibility for the arrest of Beatrice's cousins.

   Her attempt to reconcile Eddie and Catherine is brought to a halt by Rodolpho's entrance, which releases a further spasm of anger in Eddie. He brushes aside Rodolpho's impressive effort to restore good relations by offering a sincere and humble apology for his part in the family's troubles. His fumbling attempt to kiss Eddie's hand is interpreted as a sign of weakness. Rodolpho's hope that even Marco can be reconciled is dashed by Eddie's obtuse intransigence. Eddie sees Marco as the only one of the pair worthy of his attention. It is he who has shamed Eddie in front of his neighbours; nothing but a public restitution of his reputation will satisfactorily compensate Eddie for his humiliation. Only Beatrice can see that such a confrontation will lead to a bloody conclusion. Throughout the scene with Rodolpho, Beatrice has tried to appeal to reason, moving from persuasion to impassioned pleas that Eddie should accept Rodolpho's apology. Failing to get him to attend, she finally tries to confront him with what she sees as the underlying cause of his obstinacy—his continuing, unacknowledged, passion for Catherine. Both Catherine and Eddie are shocked by her outspokenness—predictably, Eddie refuses to accept that he could harbour such thoughts.

All thought of facing the truth is swept aside when Marco, perhaps believing that he has God's consent to murder, calls Eddie's name. Eddie responds almost joyfully, abandoning thoughtful analysis for a confrontation with the man who he thinks has insulted him. Rodolpho and Beatrice are swept aside as he addresses his neighbours with a speech of self-justification. Eddie appeals to the injunctions of the New Testament as a source for his behaviour. In his view he has admitted to his house strangers who have abused his hospitality. Eddie's account of what he has suffered is narrowly biased. He demands a submission from Marco which Marco cannot give. Accused of being a liar, threatened with assault and then with a knife, Marco as the challenger is forced to defend himself. As Eddie dies in Beatrice's arms, there is no sign that he feels remorse or any understanding of the sources of his actions.

Alfieri's closing speech has an enigmatic quality. People nowadays, he says, 'settle for half'. The phrase takes us back to his first speech, which looks back to the days of gangsterism, which does not seem to relate to the events we have been watching, except that in each case there was a connection with Italy. Alfieri admires Eddie, despite all that might be said, because he has 'allowed himself to be wholly known'. It is not clear in what sense Eddie has done this, unless by adhering to his own blindness and obstinacy. He has gone to the extreme in failing to know himself, so that he has become a kind of model of the blind striving of the unconscious.

Characters

Eddie

Eddie is a larger-than-life figure: authoritative, wilful and energetic. At the beginning of the play he exudes warmth; there is a close rapport between him and his niece, Catherine. He is interested in her looks and her clothes; he is proud of her development into an attractive woman, but he still thinks of her as a baby and wants to keep her from other men. He warns her about the dangers of being too friendly to others, but does not seem to realise that her growing up may affect the relationship she has with him. In his relations with his wife and with the outside world, he is serenely masterful; he jokes easily about the responsibility he is about to undertake in welcoming Beatrice's cousins into the house, but his humour has a sharp edge, perhaps covering some resentment at the trouble her family has put him to. Yet he is glad to appear generous. Eddie is a man with a rather thin surface of easy good humour; underneath, he is dogmatic, and quarrelsome. Although he loves Catherine, he expects her to live according to his expectations. He has little time for the people he lives amongst; yet he is prone to affectionate nostalgia for the work he does. He appears to be complacently satisfied with himself and his family: it is the possibility of change that upsets him. Before the cousins arrive, Eddie is horrified at the idea that anyone might betray an immigrant, but the early scenes of the play establish the fluctuations of his moods. His dislike of Rodolpho, which is triggered by the young man's interest in Catherine, is clearly deeply irrational, stirring in him prejudices against men who do not conform to his own type. At the same time, the revelation of his failed sexual relations with Beatrice raises questions about his own sexuality, even if these are not answered in the play.

The action of the play is an expansion, but scarcely an exploration, of Eddie's psyche, whose main characteristic is his willingness to tolerate in himself an explosive excess of emotion. He is also willing to entertain hypotheses about the motives of others, which he acts upon as if they were true. He is prepared to believe, and say, anything which will maintain the integrity of his family life and the sustaining warmth of his relationship with Catherine. When, finally, this aim conflicts with his picture of himself as a generous extrovert, he is willing to fight to the death to preserve the 'name' for liberalism and honour, whose limitations have been exposed by his own behaviour.

Beatrice

Beatrice begins as a compliant and submissive character, whose main aim in life is to keep Eddie happy. She is delighted that her cousins are about to arrive but is full of anxiety about their welfare. She clearly has a large reservoir of affection for Eddie and can still see him as the generous man he would like to be. When he shows mistrust or suspicion, she is always ready with a reassuring word, although she is clearly anxious to support Catherine's bid for an independent life. She is calm and sure about Catherine's ability to look after herself. She is more open to other people than Eddie; she does not have his vulnerable suspicion that they are likely to do him down. She is happy to allow him to be in charge, but, when they are alone, we are aware that she is capable of looking at him critically. She has a ready sympathy for her cousins and an interest in their ambitions. Although she tries to manage Eddie by adopting a cool, detached attitude to his verbal excesses, she is perfectly capable of standing up to him when necessary. As his wife, she expects Eddie to respect her and to treat her as the woman he has chosen to marry. She has a quietly serious view of what is due to her. She has no doubt that there is something wrong with his attitude to Catherine, and she is firm in communicating her view to Catherine that she must grow up. Hers is a voice of sanity and reason, and she refuses to be browbeaten by Eddie, but continually tries to reconcile Eddie and Catherine to the changes in their relationship. She is even ready to accept that she may have some responsibility for Eddie's state of mind. In the final scene of the play she tries to force Eddie to face the truth of his feelings for Catherine and to disengage him from his confrontation with Marco, but it is not until he is dying that Eddie acknowledges what she means to him.

Catherine

In comparison with her uncle and aunt, Catherine is a relatively passive character throughout the play. Initially, she is clearly devoted to Eddie, and depends upon his approval. She is obviously bright and hard-working, but she has no secure sense of identity. She has not begun to imagine a life apart from her aunt and uncle. She is enthusiastic about the arrival of the immigrants but is naive and idealistic about their status. She soon shows a natural interest in them, concentrating upon Rodolpho, because he is attractive and unmarried. She expresses her interest openly and excitedly, and it is soon obvious that her warm affection for Eddie has transferred to Rodolpho without difficulty. She is still vulnerable to attack from Eddie and requires Beatrice's support to understand the responsibilities of maturity. It is not until the opening scene of Act II that we see signs that she is becoming detached from Eddie: her dependence, in fact, has transferred to Rodolpho and she looks to him for support. She is, however, clear in her mind that she loves Rodolpho. When she realises that Eddie has betrayed him to the immigration authorities, she reacts with fury. She is as horrified as Eddie when Beatrice tries to make him face his feelings for her. Her last words to him are a pathetic mutter of apology for being the unwitting cause of his downfall and death. Catherine's scenes with Rodolpho are attractively written, allowing the actress opportunities to display a romantic dependence on her sweetheart, but in the rest of the play she is a charming *ingénue* whose hold on a separate identity is tenuous.

Rodolpho

Rodolpho is the more spirited and attractive of the two immigrant brothers whose arrival changes Eddie's destiny. It is he who impulsively speaks first in the street, unselfconsciously celebrating the fact of his arrival in America. It is certainly not uncharacteristic that one of his first words should be 'Imagine'. He is a ready verbaliser, eager to offer vivid little pictures of life in Italy. Although he talks in a way that suggests he is speaking a second language, he is skilful in the use of telling metaphors. If his speech-rhythms are not quite idiomatic, they are pointed and rhetorically effective. (Consider his response to Beatrice's question, 'You gotta push a taxi?'— 'Oh, sure. It's a feature in our town.' 'Feature' is not the word a native speaker would use, but Rodolpho uses it with confident emphasis.) His short, grammatically simple sentences add to the general impression he creates of ebullient and intelligent oddity. He makes jokes and is not afraid to use his own experience as a subject for them. His rapid transitions from motorbikes to messages to opera-singing emphasise the sense that he is unusual, and maybe a bit eccentric. He is an extrovert but does not appear to wish to dominate; he is, indeed, rather self-deprecating and only too anxious to be deferential when called to order. A harsh view of him would be that he is self-centred, but his egoism is softened by his charm. Masculine charm, however, finds little favour with Eddie, for whom these terms are contradictory. Rodolpho's ebullience is chilled by Eddie's apparent indifference which hardens to hostility. Rodolpho is mortified because he believes that he possesses, beneath his extravagant surface behaviour, qualities of steadiness and integrity. Ripened by his love for Catherine, they emerge most strongly in the love scene in Act II, in which he displays tenderness and affection as well as a sharp sense of realism about why he has come to America. In his wooing of Catherine he displays a mature and tender concern for the girl whose feelings he has aroused. In offering an apology to Eddie for not treating him with the respect Eddie believes is his due, he behaves sensibly and straightforwardly. He does his best to warn Eddie about how Marco is likely to take the law into his own hands. His behaviour during the course of the play dispels our initial impression that he is a lightweight character; indeed he visibly matures into a stable, resourceful, generous and reliable man, who offers a much more acceptable model of manliness than does Eddie.

Marco

Marco offers a third example of what counts as manliness. He is conventionally strong and silent. As Eddie puts it, 'Marco goes round like a man; nobody kids Marco.' He is obviously devoted to his family and speaks of his wife with deep, if restrained, affection. He is apparently more sensible than Rodolpho, whom he treats with the indulgence of an older, wiser brother. He is quick to defend him when Eddie appears to treat him badly, though Marco's challenge to Eddie at the end of Act I is unaggressive. He is polite and courteous; he seems a man of deliberation and cautious good sense. In his character, however, there is a rigidity, produced, no doubt, by the ethos of his early surroundings. He has a clear and simple view of what should happen to a man who has offended against the code of the clan. He does not allow any argument to deflect him from what he sees as his duty to punish. He is even willing to cover his intention to kill by making a statement which is liable to be misunderstood. Of all the characters in the play, Marco is the one we know least. His mind appears closed to everything except family, work and a narrow, rigorous sense of duty. His sense of self, unlike Eddie's, or Rodolpho's, is unmixed with fantasy: his singleness of vision is both impressive and frightening in its intensity.

Alfieri

Although Alfieri does take part in the action of the play, his main role is as an observer and commentator. He represents a view of law which is objective, unemotional and aware of its own limitations. When, in his final speech, he says, 'Most of the time now we settle for half and I like it better', we may suppose that he means that the legal system does not dispense absolute justice. It is content to manage an administrative system which deals with only part of the human problems which come before it. Alfieri is less a human character than a dramatic device. The actor who plays the part has to be both a character and a chorus who comments impersonally upon the action. He is honourable, upright and concerned. He has considerable insight into Eddie's problems, but his function in the play does not allow him to do more than observe.

Conclusion

A View from the Bridge is a cleverly constructed play whose episodes lead to a brilliantly effective theatrical conclusion. Many famous plays end with a fatal confrontation between two powerful men. (We need only think of *Hamlet* and *Macbeth*.) Marco and Eddie are not socially of any great consequence, but Marco, at least, represents a coherent, if narrow, morality. His belief that it is right to kill Eddie rests on the traditions of the Sicilian vendetta. Eddie has injured—even meta-phorically 'killed'—Marco's family; by depriving Marco of his livelihood, he has deprived his family of the means to live and, therefore, of life itself. He has offended against the code which demands that families should support one another.

Eddie's case against Marco is weaker: he believes that he had the right to inform on Rodolpho, because he was 'stealing' from him. But as the play makes clear, Eddie has no moral right to behave as if he 'possessed' Catherine. The word itself suggests that Eddie's secret desires for Catherine are incestuous and anti-social. It is also certain that there are no grounds for implicating Marco in whatever crime Rodolpho may be supposed to have committed. From an early stage in the play, Eddie himself has recognised the unacceptability of betraying members of the family group. Having accepted Beatrice's cousins into his house, he is obliged to protect them. Can Rodolpho's behaviour in falling in love with Catherine be held to be a breach of Eddie's hospitality?

Perhaps the answer is that behind these issues there are larger questions. The Italian brothers are cousins of Beatrice, but they are also competitors in the job market, as Mike and Louis realise. The immigrants are illegal because the immigration policies of the United States in the 1920s began to exclude categories which had previously been allowed to enter without hindrance. Some of these restrictions were made necessary by the backlog of prospective immigrants which had built up during the First World War, but they were applied in a way which barred migrants of southern- and western-European origins. Thus Italians and Greeks were less favoured than immigrants from Great Britain and northern Europe. As John A. Garraty puts it in his book *The American Nation: a History of the United States* (6th edn, 1987):

> The United States had not only closed the gates, it had abandoned the theory of the melting pot. Instead of an open, cosmopolitan society, eager to accept, in Emma Lazarus' stirring lines, the 'huddled masses yearning to breathe free, the wretched refuse' of Europe's 'teeming shore', America now became committed to preserving a homogeneous 'Anglo-Saxon' population.

These anomalies were removed by legislation in the 1960s, but they may be thought to colour Miller's play. If Eddie is representative of a section of working-class America, his attitude to strangers is ambivalent. The 'name' that Eddie has lost is just that name for generosity, for an open door to the poor of the world, which the United States had claimed.

A View from the Bridge offers a finely graded spectrum of Italians in America. The audience is invited to look, as it were, from Brooklyn Bridge on to Red Hook, from a position of privilege to a less privileged corner of New York. Alfieri, through whose eyes the action is seen, is a successfully assimilated Italian immigrant who has been able to distance himself from the struggle for existence. Eddie and his family and neighbours are at the borderline of being American. Eddie wanted to direct Catherine towards 'a different kind of people' and to work in 'maybe a lawyer's office some place in New York in one of them nice buildings'. Instead he has to watch her falling in love with an Italian immigrant who has little understanding of America and no established place on its social ladder.

On to this easily intelligible social drama, Miller has grafted much darker psychological material which has to do with the internal structure of the family itself. In the preface to the first version of the play, Miller speaks of the density of the material which it contains and which it would require many plays to exhaust. Eddie's possessiveness and his denial of it are well established. Beatrice plays a crucial role in diagnosing the strength of Eddie's feelings for Catherine, and Alfieri, in his first interview with Eddie, states the general problem which may occur when a child first wants to leave home. The failure of Eddie's sexual relationship with Beatrice is further evidence that his sexual interests may have become distorted, but despite Eddie's onstage kissing of Catherine, there is little direct evidence that his interest is incestuous. When Beatrice asserts, just before the closing episode of the play, that it is Catherine whom Eddie wants, the spectators may think that there is something forced in this accusation, that it depends too much on feelings which have not been adequately demonstrated in the action of the play. Something of the same kind may be said about the theme of homosexuality. It may be held that in kissing Rodolpho, Eddie behaves in a way which reflects badly on himself and that he harbours feelings for Rodolpho which he would never acknowledge. His preoccupation with Rodolpho's looks and voice and interests may reinforce this suspicion. Yet it is not easy to argue that this is a deeply rooted unconscious preoccupation of Eddie's. The two characters offer contrasted versions of what it is to be a man. It may suit Eddie's purpose to impugn Rodolpho's character by bringing against him the most serious accusation he can think of. But Rodolpho never for a moment gives us any reason to believe the charge is true, nor does Eddie give us reason to believe that he harbours unacknowledged homosexual feelings for Rodolpho. Of course, he may feel threatened by this alternative version of what it is to be manly. At the time the play was first staged, public discussion of homosexuality was almost unheard of; it was because the play appeared to hint at the topic that it was initially banned from the London stage. A kiss exchanged between men in public was thought indecent. When Eddie kisses Rodolpho, it is a gesture of his anger and contempt, but even this expression of emotion between two men was considered unsuitable for the stage. Eddie uses the kiss aggressively to imply that Rodolpho is 'not right', but we know there is no truth in this charge. The episode has considerable theatrical force, but it does not mean that the play raises serious questions about homosexual feelings or behaviour.

If emphasis is placed on the internal conflicts within Eddie's family, he may be seen as a man who is almost a tragic character because he has no insight into his own motivation. His ignorance of himself is such that we may well feel pity and fear, because he reminds us of a certain blindness about our motives which we can all recognise in ourselves. But there is nothing blind about his betrayal of his relatives. In choosing to take that line of action, which has been signalled many times in the play as the breach of a clearly identified social taboo, he puts himself beyond the sympathy both of his neighbours and of the audience. We may conclude, then, that despite the excellence of its construction, its theatrical power and the interest of the issues it raises, there is something unsatisfactory about a play which does not unify the public and private issues which it raises.

Part 4

Hints for study

Reading the play

The readers of this guide to Arthur Miller's play are expected to be active participants in the exciting challenge to recreate this imagined action in the theatre of their own minds, hearing the accents and tones of the actors and watching the pattern of their movements, seeing their reactions to what other characters say, noticing their disengagements or their silences, imagining what movements would best support and amplify the words the author has written. There is no end to the delicacy of such acts of imagination. Theatrical directors in real life must oversee the planning and building of a stage set, must have views on how their actors should sound, must know what clothes they would wear and what their surroundings would look like. In *Timebends* (p.13), describing the first production of his play *The Price*, Miller tells us how he went to an old aunt to borrow back the tables and chairs which had furnished the living-room of his father's house which he had been thinking of when he wrote the play. Arthur Miller's plays combine elements of realism and non-realism, but, whatever their form, they are rooted in a strong sense of particular places and of particular people. Imaginative readers of his plays will always be eager to track down the historical, social and biographical facts out of which his plays have been composed.

Essentially, however, the view of the play taken by both director and reader demands a close reading of the text and depends upon it. The method of analysis pursued so far has been to find scene-divisions within each act and to notice that within each scene there is a patterned structure which generates from the interplay of the characters an emotional effect which provides the basis for the next section of the play. This does not mean that the sections are linked by an unbroken cumulative flow of feeling. The structure of the play allows for gradations of intensity. There are climaxes where the characters interact in a tense and emphatic way, but these may be followed by sections where the impetus, or pace, of the action is slacker, less focused. It is the combination of these effects that produces the sense we have of the characteristic direction, or trajectory, of the action which eventually leads to a particular conclusion. To look even more closely at how these effects are produced, we may turn to consider the third episode of the fourth scene in Act I when Rodolpho and Catherine have just returned from the cinema.

The two young people enter to the ambiguous laughter of the longshoremen, who have just been talking about Rodolpho. There should be a moment or two on stage when Eddie appears lonely, disturbed and rather forlorn, before Catherine and Rodolpho enter, their happiness bringing his mood into sharp relief. Catherine is excited and her exclamations are, as it were, invitations to him to share their pleasure. This cannot succeed because she is inviting him to share her memory of the good time she has had with Rodolpho, so the invitation to share can only remind him that he has been excluded. Practically, she is asking Eddie for his sympathy and approval, but she may in fact rouse feelings of jealousy in him. Eddie smiles, and no doubt turns to meet them, but he is not interested in hearing about the film. He wants to know where they have been, and the question implies a doubt as to whether they have kept within the limits he appears to have set before they went out. Asking such a question implies that he has authority over Catherine and that he wants to know whether she has been obedient. It is not surprising that Catherine shows her anger in her reply.

Retreating before this spark of anger, Eddie turns to Rodolpho, giving him a reason for his concern, not apparently noticing that it suggests Rodolpho's presence would not be a help in danger, almost implying that he would lead Catherine into undesirable company. Rodolpho's reply ignores these implications. He probably does not understand them. Where Eddie associates Broadway with beggars and prostitutes (the word 'tramp' carries a hint of each of these meanings), Rodolpho thinks of the romance of theatre and opera. The divergent associations of the two men imply differences in character which are grounded in differences of culture and temperament. To see Broadway will fulfil a childhood dream for Rodolpho; to walk there with Catherine will crown it with the glamour of adult romance. Eddie simply cannot respond to these remarks. He has his own quasi-romantic flirtation with Catherine, and to notice Rodolpho's relationship with her would be to diminish his own.

Eddie's attempt to detach the lovers from one another meets with no success. They are too full of the wonder of being together. Rodolpho's 'she teaches me' has all the emphasis of his gratitude for what Catherine has brought him; it expresses respect, as well as warm affection. For a moment Catherine tries to draw Eddie into the current of her relationship with Rodolpho; we can see how she has tried to empathise with his life in Italy, though his stories of life there seem strange and remote in comparison with his enthusiasm for New York. But when Rodolpho himself tries to enter the rapport which exists between Eddie and Catherine, he is rebuffed. There is no hope that Eddie will accept him as a suitor for Catherine or as a friend for himself.

When Rodolpho leaves them, Catherine continues to speak for him. It is a measure of the intractability of the situation that Eddie accuses Catherine of denying him the recognition that she begs him to give to Rodolpho. Of course, there is no parallel between these relationships: Rodolpho is seeking the approval that a father might give to the young man who is courting his daughter. When Eddie uses the same words as Catherine to describe his own case, we are struck by the inappropriateness of the demand he is making. It is not true that she does not talk to him, unless we mean by 'talk' a response too intimate to be wholly proper between an uncle and a niece. The stage direction says that Eddie envelopes Catherine with his eyes and tries to smile. Such feelings are disproportionate; they are immature because they reverse the natural dependence which might exist between guardian and child. Eddie depends on Catherine for his happiness; if she transfers her affection to another man, the light of his life goes out. In the words that follow we can see the flickering of Eddie's spirit. He concedes that Catherine's new status has disorientated him. It is not that she does not talk to him; he does not know how to talk to her; and he is losing contact with her. Or does he mean that he is losing control over her?

None of the undertones of these speeches by Eddie have been understood by Catherine. She takes them at face value, oblivious of what they say of his attitude to herself and of his dependence upon her. She still believes it is a question of his approval of Rodolpho. In the crucial little exchange where Catherine says:

> . . .What's the matter? You don't like him?
> [*Slight pause.*]
> EDDIE: [*turns to her*]: You like him, Katie?
> CATHERINE: [*with a blush but holding her ground*]: Yeah. I like him.
> EDDIE: [*—his smile goes*]: You like him.

we can see that it is not the fact that it is Rodolpho Catherine is attracted to, it is the whole issue of Catherine's liking for another man that Eddie is questioning. Eddie is not here being the adult who is trying to be clear about the real state of mind of the child for whom he is responsible. He is a jealous rival. The second 'You like him' must display Eddie's sullen disappointment: he lightly emphasises the word 'like', making it clear that it is her liking which hurts.

Having lost the struggle to establish intimacy with her—notice how he uses the diminutive of her name to do this—he launches his attack on Rodolpho. Miller manages to establish a tiny play on the word 'bless'. When Catherine says that Rodolpho blesses Eddie, she thinks of blessing as an active process, but when Eddie uses the word, he thinks of it as a process of which he is, or should be, the beneficiary. Rodolpho's attitude confers no feeling of blessing; Eddie is unmoved by what the young man says he feels. His attack on Rodolpho is directed exactly to the emotional tone that was established when the young couple entered. It is precisely Rodolpho's feelings of respect for Catherine which Eddie now attempts to put in question. He tries to convince Catherine that Rodolpho is not interested in her, but in becoming an American citizen by marrying her. This telling climax is built up in small stages so that by the time Catherine rushes into the house, shouting her disbelief, we have seen her move from serenity to distress, just as we have seen Eddie move from impotence to disappointment to a malicious triumph of denigration.

Further analysis at this level of delicacy would help to reveal the subtle dynamics of the text. The reader/director is compelled to think of the broad rhythms of the play, of the changes in relationship between the characters, as being borne along on the subtle fluctuations of mood from speech to speech. In the episode which completes the scene we have been analysing, Beatrice counters Eddie's 'Why don't you straighten her out?' with a syntactically parallel 'When are you going to leave her alone?' Each is a question, each refers to Catherine: the first asks Beatrice to intervene in Catherine's life; the second asks Eddie when he is going to stop interfering with her life. Beatrice's response catches Eddie in full flight, as a set of buffers might catch a railway train, and the action of the play is put into reverse as she now encourages Catherine to stand up to Eddie. So Eddie's 'The guy is no good' becomes 'The guy ain't right' in the following scene with Alfieri, switching the sense from a defect of character to a defect of personality, even of physiology, and from a moral defect to a sexual deficiency.

In the scene with Alfieri, Eddie begins with the suspicion he has first broached in the previous scene, namely, that Rodolpho wants Catherine so that he can become an American citizen. It is only when this line of argument fails that he moves by tiny steps to suggesting that Rodolpho is homosexual, a word he does not use. It is worth analysing in detail the steps in the transaction: first, the hushed pause which signals some embarrassing revelation, the plea for confidentiality, the physical signs of Rodolpho's difference from Eddie's standard notion of manliness—the blond hair, the light build, the tenor voice—the aspects of his physical type that seem unmanly, and the willingness to help Catherine with her dress, all of which culminates for Eddie in his assessment of the humiliating reaction of the neighbours. Embedded in the speech are hints of Eddie's own muddled sexuality: Rodolpho was 'so sweet there, like an angel—you could kiss him he was so sweet'; Eddie cannot bear the thought of 'that guy layin' his hands on her'. Pushed further, he might be thought to be wondering why Catherine should be loved by 'a punk', like Rodolpho, rather than by a man, like himself. If the thought is unexpressed in the play, it is confirmed when Eddie says, at the end of the scene, 'He's stealing from me.' Alfieri does not, of course, comment on the suggestion, if it is there, that Eddie has found Rodolpho attractive, but he does seize upon Eddie's interest in Catherine which forms the basis of his response to Eddie. However, even when he puts the point bluntly ('She can't marry you can she?'), Eddie cannot hear what is being said. This episode is crucial because it forms the basis for the first confrontation with Rodolpho, which includes Catherine's first open defiance of Eddie, and Marco's first counter-challenge. These constitute the culmination of the first act and they in turn prepare the way for the next encounter between Eddie, Catherine and Rodolpho which takes place at the beginning of the second act. The object of further study of the play would be to map in fine detail the way in which Miller has linked climax to climax, episode to episode and speech to speech so that the whole action of the play appears inevitably generated by the movement of its smallest constituents.

Some specimen questions

(1) In *A View from the Bridge* what the characters say is more important than anything they do. Do you agree?

(2) 'There is nothing inevitable about the denouement of *A View from the Bridge*; it is the accidental result of an irrational impulse.' Do you think this a valid comment on the play?

(3) How true in your view is Alfieri's remark that Eddie Carbone 'allowed himself to be wholly known'?

(4) How would you support the view that *A View from the Bridge* is a play about the damage done by industrial society to individual values?

(5) 'In *A View from the Bridge* Miller has tried to make a hero out of a man who has no redeeming qualities.' Do you agree?

(6) 'The interesting question posed by *A View from the Bridge* is how far aggression is a necessary attribute of manliness.' Discuss.

(7) 'In the society of *A View from the Bridge* women are dependent on men; their role is to serve and suffer.' Do you agree with this assessment? Are there any signs in the play of ways out of such sexual stereotyping?

(8) Why does Eddie take such pains to convince others that Rodolpho is 'not right'? What is your estimation of Rodolpho?

A sample answer

(6) 'The interesting question posed by *A View from the Bridge* is how far aggression is a necessary attribute of manliness.' Discuss.

'Being a man' is central to Eddie Carbone's idea of himself. He is sharply contrasted with the women in his life. In the first scene of the play he displays a keen interest in the appearance of his niece, Catherine, expressing his views freely on her hair, the length of her skirt and the way she walks down the street; but the reason for his interest is his acute awareness of the feelings she might arouse in other men. His own feelings for her are expressed in an attitude of protectiveness which produces hostility towards those who might threaten her. In the course of the play it becomes clear that Eddie is also afraid that his control over Catherine might be threatened too, although this fact is not recognised by Eddie himself. From the beginning of the play Eddie's habit is to control and dominate: he is strong, he is assertive, he is the breadwinner, the organiser; it is he who has a life outside, which in generous moments he shares with the women of the house. Looked at from another point of view, however, it might be argued that his life is equally determined by them: he lives to protect them, even if his protection is also a limitation of their lives, and even if, in the case of Beatrice, it fails to satisfy all her needs.

There are aspects of Eddie's aggressiveness which are not accounted for simply by his desire to protect his family. Some of the anger is directed against Beatrice, who is willing to let Catherine go, just as it is directed against Alfieri, when he makes the same suggestion in Act I [Scene 5] and probes too near the feelings for Catherine which Eddie has hidden from himself. It is clear, too, that Catherine does not want to be protected from the world of work or from the chance to form close relationships with another man. The play raises questions about the necessity for Eddie's protectiveness; it also raises questions about the integrity of those feelings. Might it not be the case that Eddie's aggressiveness springs partly from a desire to manipulate and control, partly from a wish to frighten off others from what he wants to keep for himself—namely, Catherine? If this is true, the role of Beatrice in the family is to justify and divert suspicion from Eddie's relationship with Catherine. Unconsciously, Eddie is using Beatrice as a shield. For Eddie, then, the role of a father implies possessiveness and domination, opposition to which produces anger. We do not associate him with sympathy, tenderness, generosity or love.

Rodolpho offers a very different image of manliness. He is not afraid to seem a little inferior to Catherine: 'She teaches me', he says in Act I [Scene 4]. Rodolpho represents a world of interests and pleasures rather than of work. As Eddie says of him disparagingly, 'He sings, he cooks, he could make dresses.' There is no place for Rodolpho on the waterfront, in Eddie's view. In fact, there is nothing effeminate about Rodolpho: his singing is part of Italian popular culture, his cooking is part of the work that has to be done on board ship, and his dressmaking is a purely private service which he does for Catherine. He has no experience of the ritualised aggression of the boxing match, but he acts promptly when Eddie kisses Catherine in the first scene of Act II, where he displays a kind of astonished outrage rather than anger. He is able to express his intention to marry Catherine in a controlled and deliberate way. It is only under Eddie's taunting insinuations, which are enacted in the degrading kiss he forces on him, that Rodolpho gives way to his feelings of rage. At the end of the play he is prepared to be reconciled with Eddie and warns him against the approach of Marco. When we compare the words and actions of Eddie and Rodolpho, we must conclude that it is not necessary to be aggressive in order to be self-assertive.

A final test of the relationship between aggressiveness and manliness may be seen in the character of Marco. It is his terrifying shout of 'Eddie Carbone' that prepares the audience for the fatal outcome of the play. In many ways Marco resembles Eddie; his life, too, is dedicated to work and to his family. But the narrowness of his life has a purity which is quite different from Eddie's. Marco's life is governed by an ideal of self-sacrifice rather than a desire for self-gratification. Even his resolve to kill is determined by the code of his society and is fortified, however misguidedly, by prayer. His behaviour is not tainted by the secret perversity which rules Eddie's actions, but its narrow-minded intensity, supported by a belief in revenge, is scarcely meant to be admired. In the end, those two primitive views of what it is to be a man cancel one another out. What remains is the modest image of tender, affectionate, thoughtful domesticated man with which Rodolpho leaves us.

Part 5

Suggestions for further reading

The text

A View from the Bridge: Two One-Act Plays by Arthur Miller, Viking, New York, 1955. One-act version of the text, includes a preface by the author.

Collected Plays: Volume I, Viking, New York, 1957; reissued by Secker and Warburg, London, 1974. Two-act version of the text, includes a preface by the author.

A View from the Bridge and *All My Sons*, Penguin, Harmondsworth, 1961. Widely available edition.

Miller Plays: One, (Methuen's World Dramatists Series) Methuen, London, 1988.

Other works by the author

Focus, 1945; *All My Sons*, 1947; *Death of a Salesman*, 1949; *An Enemy of the People*, 1950; *The Crucible*, 1953; *After the Fall*, 1964; *The Price*, 1968; *The Archbishop's Ceiling*, 1977; *The American Clock*, 1980; *Timebends: A Life*, 1987.

Critical works

BIGSBY, C. W. E.: *A Critical Introduction to Twentieth-Century American Drama*, Vol. 2, Cambridge University Press, Cambridge, 1984.

BIGSBY, C. W. E.: *File on Miller*, (Writer Files) Methuen, London, 1987.

CARSON, NEIL: *Arthur Miller*, (Macmillan Modern Dramatists) Macmillan, London, 1982.

HAYMAN, RONALD: *Arthur Miller*, Unger, New York, 1972.

MARTIN, ROBERT A. (ED.): *Arthur Miller: New Perspectives*, Prentice-Hall, Englewood Cliffs, 1982.

MOSS, LEONARD: *Arthur Miller*, Twayne, New York, 1967.

ROUDANÉ, MATTHEW C. (ED.): *Conversations with Arthur Miller*, University of Mississippi Press, Jackson and London, 1987.

WELLAND, DENNIS: *Arthur Miller*, Oliver and Boyd, London, 1961.

WELLAND, DENNIS: *Miller: A Study of his Plays*, Eyre Methuen, London, revised edition 1983.
WELLAND, DENNIS: *Miller: The Playwright*, 3rd edition, Methuen, London, 1985.

The author of these notes

IAN MILLIGAN was educated at the University of Glasgow where he gained the degrees of MA and MEd. After teaching in the Royal High School, Edinburgh, he became a lecturer in English at Moray House College of Education, Edinburgh. He now lectures in the Department of English Studies at the University of Stirling. He has published articles on education, on the teaching of literature and on nineteenth- and twentieth-century literature. He is the author of York Notes on Jane Austen's *Northanger Abbey*, Anthony Trollope's *Barchester Towers*, Richard Hughes's *A High Wind in Jamaica*, L. P. Hartley's *The Shrimp and the Anemone* and the York Handbooks, *The English Novel* and *Studying Jane Austen*. He has also written the Macmillan Master Guide on *Howards End* by E. M. Forster and *The Novel in English: An Introduction*, Macmillan, London, 1983; 1987.

York Handbooks: list of titles

YORK HANDBOOKS form a companion series to York Notes and are designed to meet the wider needs of students of English and related fields. Each volume is a compact study of a given subject area, written by an authority with experience in communicating the essential ideas to students at all levels.

AN A.B.C. OF SHAKESPEARE
by P. C. BAYLEY

A DICTIONARY OF BRITISH AND IRISH AUTHORS
by ANTONY KAMM

A DICTIONARY OF LITERARY TERMS (Second Edition)
by MARTIN GRAY

ENGLISH GRAMMAR
by LORETO TODD

ENGLISH POETRY
by CLIVE T. PROBYN

AN INTRODUCTION TO AUSTRALIAN LITERATURE
by TREVOR JAMES

AN INTRODUCTION TO LINGUISTICS
by LORETO TODD

AN INTRODUCTION TO LITERARY CRITICISM
by RICHARD DUTTON

AN INTRODUCTORY GUIDE TO ENGLISH LITERATURE
by MARTIN STEPHEN

THE METAPHYSICAL POETS
by TREVOR JAMES

PREPARING FOR EXAMINATIONS IN ENGLISH LITERATURE
by NEIL McEWAN

READING THE SCREEN: AN INTRODUCTION TO FILM STUDIES
by JOHN IZOD

STUDYING CHAUCER
by ELISABETH BREWER

STUDYING JANE AUSTEN
by IAN MILLIGAN

STUDYING SHAKESPEARE
by MARTIN STEPHEN *and* PHILIP FRANKS

STUDYING THOMAS HARDY
by LANCE ST JOHN BUTLER

WOMEN WRITERS IN ENGLISH LITERATURE
by JANE STEVENSON